CITYSPOTS
BRATISLAVA

Thomas Cook

D042402Z

WHAT'S IN YOUR GUIDEBOOK?

Independent authors Impartial up-to-date information from our travel experts who meticulously source local knowledge.

Experience Thomas Cook's 165 years in the travel industry and guidebook publishing enriches every word with expertise you can trust.

Travel know-how Thomas Cook has thousands of staff working around the globe, all living and breathing travel.

Editors Travel-publishing professionals, pulling everything together to craft a perfect blend of words, pictures, maps and design.

You, the traveller We deliver a practical, no-nonsense approach to information, geared to how you really use it.

CITYSPOTS
BRATISLAVA

Written by Wendy Wrangham
Updated by Kristina Konikova

Published by Thomas Cook Publishing
A division of Thomas Cook Tour Operations Limited
Company registration No: 3772199 England
The Thomas Cook Business Park, 9 Coningsby Road
Peterborough PE3 8SB, United Kingdom
Email: books@thomascook.com, Tel: +44 (0)1733 416477
www.thomascookpublishing.com

Produced by The Content Works Ltd
Aston Court, Kingsmead Business Park, Frederick Place
High Wycombe, Bucks HP11 1LA
www.thecontentworks.com

Series design based on an original concept by Studio 183 Limited

ISBN: 978-1-84848-077-3

First edition © 2007 Thomas Cook Publishing
This second edition © 2009 Thomas Cook Publishing
Text © Thomas Cook Publishing
Maps © Thomas Cook Publishing/PCGraphics (UK) Limited
Transport map © Communicarta Limited

Series Editor: Lucy Armstrong
Production/DTP: Steven Collins

Printed and bound in Spain by GraphyCems

Cover photography (Bratislava Castle) © Ian Shaw/Alamy

CONTENTS

SYMBOLS KEY

The following symbols are used throughout this book:

@ address ① telephone ⓦ website address ⓛ opening times
Ⓝ public transport connections ① important

The following symbols are used on the maps:

i information office		■ points of interest	
✈ airport		O city	
✚ hospital		O large town	
⬡ police station		○ small town	
▤ bus station		═ motorway	
▤ railway station		— main road	
Ⓜ metro		— minor road	
✝ cathedral		— railway	
❶ numbers denote featured cafés & restaurants			

Hotels and restaurants are graded by approximate price as follows:
£ budget price **££** mid-range price **£££** expensive

▶ *Bratislavský hrad (Bratislava Castle) seen from the Old Town Hall tower*

INTRODUCING
Bratislava

Introduction

It is an acknowledged truth that Slovaks have a world-beating ice hockey team, but put them on the rink with the Czech Republic and they tend to lose. However, there are many changes and developments afoot in Bratislava and they all point to one thing: Bratislava, the little big city, is no longer playing second fiddle to Prague.

For centuries Bratislava held a key position sitting in the centre of Europe and on the River Danube. It has held numerous names (including Wratisslaburgium and Istropolis), been ruled by the Hungarians, unsuccessfully besieged by the Turks, hardly beautified by the Communists and today it is being explored by everyone.

Bratislava lies on the border with Hungary and Austria thus producing two claims to fame: it is the only capital bordering two nations; and it and Vienna are the two closest capital cities in the world. The Small Carpathian Mountains dwindle into the city and give rise to excellent wine country and rural pursuits in the suburbs.

Culturally, Bratislava has hosted Mozart and Liszt. The National Theatre and Philharmonic Orchestra attract audiences for superlative performances and value for money. Galleries, museums and castles abound, laying testament to its long and varied cultural and historical past. And yet, Bratislava has a decidedly modern atmosphere with a social scene that meanders wildly between turn-of-the-century cafés, sleek chic restaurants and clubs in nuclear bunkers.

The mélange is fairly neatly contained in an area that can be easily walked, although trams and trolleybuses ply their trade to distant sights and sounds. The twists and turns of cobbled streets can and invariably do lead to another discovery or even just a seat to sit and watch the world go by.

The vineyards, castles, ski slopes, spas and beautiful countryside will tempt you to stay longer, but if your stay is limited in length, you will still discover a city steeped in history, littered with palaces and pulsing to a vibrant beat.

⬤ *Art is a common feature of Bratislava's streets*

When to go

SEASONS & CLIMATE

Situated as it is in Central Europe with little elevation, Bratislava's climate is continental with warm, often hot, summers punctuated by sharp thunderstorms. The cold winters usually produce snowfalls with the coldest temperatures occurring around January. Bratislava does have four seasons, although spring and autumn can be non-existent as daily temperatures tend to fluctuate from 22°C (72°F) to around freezing in one day at the turn of the seasons.

The High Tatras Mountains to the north gratefully receive copious snowfall for the resorts but this has also caused avalanches. The unpredictability of the mountain weather is mirrored to a lesser degree in Bratislava so a hat, sunscreen, sweater and umbrella are all useful day pack items.

Bratislavans head out of the city most weekends to their *chata* (holiday home). As ever, summer has many more tourists

● *Visit the bustling Christmas markets for festive food and drink*

than winter. September and October see national and cultural monuments inundated with kids on school trips before winter arrives and many sights and services close. However, the Christmas markets and outdoor New Year celebrations are a wonderful time to see Bratislava at its decorated best.

ANNUAL EVENTS

January
Orthodox Christmas falls on 6 January and the season doesn't officially end until then.

February
Carnival is the season (Feb–Mar) of excess before and after belts are tightened for Lent. Experience music, food and performers on the streets of the Old Town.

March
Jam along to Living Blues, an annual international festival of rhythm and blues.

April
Take an alternate route to Bratislava from Devín Castle with a road race open to all ages, all abilities and all nationalities.

May
May Day heralds spring, the coming of summer and the sap rising. The European Days of Summer cultural festival includes music, dance and recreational activities. International Museum & Gallery Day (18 May) sees Bratislava's venues open their doors for free.

June

The International Water Sprite Festival wets the city around the Danube and Old Town. The **Beer Festival** (ⓦ www.junifest.sk) kicks off with cannon fire and hardly calms down thereafter. Events from the Summer Cultural Festival (see page 14) also begin.

July

Festival of Historical Combat, Music, Dance and Crafts at Devín Castle (July and August).

September

A superb three-day Coronation Festival takes Bratislava to its royal past as hundreds of people in period costume re-enact the Coronation procession. Enjoy festivities, eat roasts, marvel at knights, horsemen and fireworks as streets come alive with thousands of revellers.

The region also raises glasses of *burciak* (young wine) for the young wine festival (see page 110).

October

More music with **Bratislava Jazz Days** (ⓦ www.bjd.sk). Meanwhile, the prestigious **Bratislava Musical Festival** (ⓦ www.bhsfestival.sk), which began 40 years ago, continues to collect international performers and accolades.

November

From late October, Bratislava's galleries, cafés and streets are covered in photography for **Photography Month** (ⓦ www.fotofo.sk), Central Europe's oldest and most influential photo festival. The region gets its skirts in a flap for the Flamenco festival.

December
Traditional and warming food and drinks spice up the stalls and events of the Christmas markets, and concerts and fireworks herald the New Year at *Silvestre* (31 December). The **Next Festival** (ⓦ www.nextfestival.sk) showcases multimedia musicians, while the **International Film Festival** (ⓦ www.iffbratislava.sk) lights up Bratislava's screens.

PUBLIC HOLIDAYS
New Year and Day of Establishment of the Slovak Republic 1 Jan
Epiphany and Christmas of Orthodox Christians 6 Jan
May Day 1 May
Liberation of the Republic 8 May
St Cyril & St Methodius Day 5 July
Slovak National Uprising Day 29 Aug
Slovak Constitution Day 1 Sept
Our Lady of Seven Sorrows 15 Sept
All Saints' Day 1 Nov
Velvet Revolution & Students' Day 17 Nov
Christmas Eve 24 Dec
Christmas Day 25 Dec
Boxing Day 26 Dec

Summer Cultural Festival

It's not the hills that are alive with the sound of music from late June to late September each year, it's the city, castle and river of Bratislava. The Summer Cultural Festival was inaugurated in 1975. Through the years, it has grown into a series of 200 presentations on 21 stages, featuring a cast of more than 1,500 from 20 countries. It's no wonder it attracts almost 70,000 visitors.

Diverse theatre, cinema, dance and music (from classical to gospel via blue grass, for example) attract audiences of all ages and interests. Sting once performed here, circus actors from Ukraine have fascinated kids and adults alike, and wine sampling adds to the atmosphere. Every summer, Bratislava offers a plethora of events, no matter what your interests.

One of the highlights is Viva Musica!, a modern festival of classical music. Bratislava Castle courtyard hosts the Summer Shakespeare Festival. The corresponding Prague Castle Shakespeare Festival brings performances here and vice versa, putting the Bard's genius on a breathtaking stage. The castle concert hall echoes with the plaintive sounds of the Days of Organ Music and other concerts featuring renowned Slovak artists. The streets and squares of the Old Town bop to the beat of Celtic or Flamenco music, while the Old Town Hall and Zoo host popular children's events.

International and local visitors experience traditional Slovak folk music, culture, costumes and pastimes, such as fencing and dancing, while participants from countries as diverse as Taiwan and the USA introduce their cultural and musical heritage to the streets of Bratislava.

Slovak Constitution Day on 1 September is a particularly poignant day of proud celebration, but no matter how long or short a time you have, Bratislava defies you not to find its Summer Cultural Festival a feast for all senses.

🔺 *A performance of the Slovak Philharmonic Orchestra*

History

Bratislava has hosted a settlement since the Iron Age, when the cliff site of Devín Castle was first settled. The local Celts were subdued by the Romans, who located their Limes Romanus defensive fortress at Devín in the first century AD, and the Slavs arrived in the late fifth century AD. By the 14th century, Bratislava had become one of the most important towns and castles of the Hungarian kingdom, and its fortified position held off sieges aplenty.

Bratislava's position on the border of three countries is testament to its muddled history. Rule had constantly fluctuated between Austria and Hungary with Polish and Jagiellonian kings entering the fray every now and then.

This rivalry between Hungary and Austria continued until 1526, when the Turks defeated the Hungarians and occupied Buda. The Hungarian kingdom became part of the Austrian (Habsburg) monarchy and in 1536 Bratislava (or Pressburg as it was known at the time) became the capital of Royal Hungary.

In 1808 Napoleon besieged Bratislava and bombed Devín. The 19th century saw a rise of the Slovak National Movement, with Ľudovít Štúr and friends codifying the Slovak language and leading the short-lived 1848 Revolution. Following the 1918 declaration of Czechoslovakia as an independent state, Bratislava revolted and was declared a free town. However, early 1919 saw Czech soldiers march on the city and bring it into the fold. Later that year, Bratislava officially became the city's name.

During World War II, Czechoslovakia was divided into two Nazi puppet states until liberation by the Red Army in April 1945. A few years later the Communist Party gained power. Alexander

Dubček, the Slovak politician briefly leader of Czechoslovakia (1968–9), attempted his famous reform of the Communist regime (Prague Spring), but failed. His speech in Bratislava on 15 November 1989 inspired student demonstrations against the Communists, and the Velvet Revolution took place on 17 November.

On 31 December 1992 Czechoslovakia was formally divided into two independent states. Since then Bratislava has been Slovakia's capital.

The 21st century has been a time of massive development since the country joined the EU in 2004. On 1 January 2009, Slovakia adopted the euro as its official currency.

⬤ *The earliest settlements were around Devín Castle*

Lifestyle

The Slovak Republic is still emerging from the yoke of the Communist Party, and there is a distinct difference in lifestyle between the older generation used to the pervasive power of the regime and the youth, who have few cultural differences to most people the world over of the same age.

This disparity is obvious in friendliness and language ability. Older people can seem cold and offer German as an alternate language, while young Bratislavans are global citizens with a growing knowledge of English. A cheery *dobrý deň* (hello, literally 'good day') and *do videnia* (goodbye) will often cause a smile to light up a Slovak's face, and to really score points with the locals use *ahoj* (as sailors say) and *čau* (like the Italian ciao) for 'hello' and 'goodbye'. *Prosím* (please) and *ďakujem* (thank you) complete your basic vocabulary. One oddity you'll have to get used to is that the Slovak word for 'yes' – *áno* – is shortened to no, which is rather confusing. 'No' is actually *nie*.

The work day is usually from around 09.00 to 17.00 (finishing earlier for those who work in the state sector). Breakfast is something like bread with cheese and/or ham and/or jam, or muesli with yoghurt and tea or coffee. Lunch tends to be on the early side. Restaurants and buffets run excellent lunch deals from 11.00–15.00. The day's meals end with a hearty dinner at home, at a restaurant or at the pub.

The notion that the Slovakians are a hard-drinking nation of back-slapping beer-quaffers is completely out of date (and, indeed, was not really accurate in the first place). The pub has an important place in local social life, but you're just as likely to see locals with their pinkies at right angles to an espresso cup as a glass or ten of the falling-down lotion. These days, alcohol is enjoyed as a social lubricant rather than a breakfast-time staple. Bratislava also now has its fair share of metrosexuals who would rather die than get beer on their Blackberry.

Slovaks are generally hospitable and friendly, unless you give them cause not to be – British stag parties take note.

● *Relaxing with a beer is the national pastime*

Culture

In the past, it seems many people came to Bratislava on the traditional Grand Tour, on the way to or from Prague, Budapest and Vienna. However, people are now discovering that Bratislava is a destination in itself. Little wonder with such a chequered and extensive history!

Traditional folk music, costume and culture have remained an important facet of Slovakian life, and folkloric performances occur all over the country, usually during summer. Slovakia's royal and aristocratic heritage still attracts tourists to Bratislava, and the region continues to produce objects and events aligned to these times. Modra is well known for traditional ceramic-making, and castles host historical festival days. Musically too, Bratislava has benefited hugely from Austria and Hungary's classical tradition. Both Mozart and Liszt performed in palaces here, while the composer J N Hummel was born here before moving to Austria to continue his work.

Austrians continue to flock to Bratislava for musical evenings, where the exterior beauty of the National Theatre and National Philharmonic buildings are mimicked by the myriad talents on stage, from chamber music to opera, drama and ballet. The prices are distinctly non-Western European, and a visit to the city should involve a foray into Bratislava's musical and theatrical heritage. Live music of all genres can be heard in clubs, restaurants and venues all over the city, but it is the summer months and festivals that really give these players their stage.

Bratislava has as many museums of various sizes as it has seen occupiers, and these fountains of historical fact exist in

◆ *The National Theatre has an international reputation for quality productions*

similarly historical houses, palaces and castles. The architecture of Bratislava, while not as classically golden as Prague's, has a complex Gothic, baroque and rococo heritage. That said, the Communists had no qualms about tearing down historical and religious sections of the city to make way for their calculated structural projects such as Nový most and Petržalka. All museums in the Slovak Republic are closed on Mondays.

Bratislava's art scene is not as renowned as its music scene, but there are numerous galleries showing religious and secular art from history as well as local and international contemporary artists. The National Gallery may not have any of the artistic wonders of the world, but the exhibits are a representative showcase of the porous borders of Bratislava's cultural identity.

Again, Bratislava is emerging from its 'older brother' syndrome and making its mark on the world's radar, free from influence from Moscow or Prague. The city, though, is still trying to shake off the cloak of drab, grey Eastern Europe that Hollywood refuses to let go of.

▶ *Napoleon surveys Hlavné námestie (Main Square)*

MAKING THE MOST OF
Bratislava

Shopping

Bratislava's changing persona from provincial town to vibrant European capital city is obvious in the vast disparity of shopping opportunities. Local shops are very specific – although the veg shop, the meat shop and the bread shop did unite somewhat as the local *potraviny*, until the behemoth Tesco arrived and showed them exactly what a supermarket could be. This central Tesco now appears a mere throwback to Bratislava's past when you visit the ultra-modern malls of Aupark, Avion and Polus, which are popping up all over the suburbs and filled with the usual IKEAs, cinema multiplexes and retailers.

The historic centre is gradually attracting high-end retailers and, eventually, Bratislava will look like Paris or Prague, with the same boutiques and labels tempting shoppers. At the moment, there is no single area or street that is becoming the retail hub, although Obchodná – literally 'shops' in Slovak – is enticing regional chains to its newly pedestrianised quarter.

Souvenirs and folk objects (wood, ceramics, glass, wire sculptures) are doing brisk business for their unique value, and the market squares of old Pressburg continue a brisk trade today with stalls selling everything from tacky t-shirts to expertly crafted tin soldiers. If you are here at Christmas, then the large markets, though becoming more and more commercialised, should satisfy all your present-giving needs.

For a look at the way locals shop – although many stalls are run by Vietnamese – head to Miletičova open air market (which is open every day except for Sunday) where you can buy anything from pickled cabbage to a pair of jeans.

◆ The place to pick up an authentic souvenir

USEFUL SHOPPING PHRASES

How much does ... cost?
Koľko stojí ...?
Koly-koh stow-yee ...?

I'm just looking. Thank you.
Len sa pozerám. Ďakujem.
Lensa pozaam. Dyakuh-yem.

My size is ...
Mám číslo ...
Maam cheeslo ...

I'd like ...
Potrebujem ...
Poh-trebuhyem ...

Do you accept credit cards?
Môžem platiť úverovou kartou?
Muo-zhem plah-tyity ooveh-rovohw kar-tohw?

For a quality gift that almost everyone would love to receive, drop into one of Bratislava's wine shops for an excellent bottle of Slovak wine. Better still, visit the Small Carpathian wine country to buy at source – see page 110. Wherever you buy, it's a good idea to sample some variations.

Eating & drinking

The days of Italian cuisine being a plate of spaghetti with ketchup and a vegetarian menu consisting of fried cheese are long gone as Bratislava's palate broadens to involve all variety of ethnic, haute and fusion cuisine.

Bars, cafés and restaurants come in all shapes and sizes, but you will find most places serve food – from a little something to go with your beer such as *utopenec* (pickled sausage) to half a spit-roasted pig. Slovak cuisine is traditionally non-vegetarian, heavy, hearty and rib-sticking. The national dish is a delicious mix of *halušky* (potato dumplings) with *bryndza* (a sheep's milk cheese) scattered with fried bacon. A less rich version is *strapačky*, which is *halušky* with sauerkraut. In addition to the usual pork, chicken and beef, local cuisine makes great use of duck, goose and game, usually in rich gravy and served with dumplings. The autumnal feast of *husacina* (stone-oven-roast goose) served with *burčiak* (young wine) is not to be missed if you are here for the season.

Slovak fast food consists of unsophisticated fried items: *lokše* are potato pancakes served sweet or as an accompaniment to

---

PRICE CATEGORIES

Price ratings in this book are based on the approximate price of a three-course meal for one person, excluding drinks but including tax.

£ up to €10   **££** €10–35   **£££** over €35

dinner and slathered with dripping. *Langoše*, a greasy fried dough pizza dolloped with ketchup, cheese and garlic sauce, seems only to be savoured by locals, but the ubiquitous *pirôžky* windows serve up a sweet doughnut for a very reasonable price. One glaring odd man out in unhealthy fast food is the Slovak vegetarian buffet, where you join the queue, order, pay, then take your plate. Try **Divesta** (£ ⓐ Laurínska 8 ⓣ 02 5443 3658), where the long line quickly dwindles.

Bageta, or *richman*, are the mayonnaise-filled sandwiches you'll see folk munching on all over the place. A good spot for these are the windows on Mariánska, which seem to be open all the time – including weekends.

⬤ *Just one of the myriad brands of beer consumed in Slovakia*

NA ZDRAVIE!

If you are eager to sample some Slovak beers, you'll need to know which ones are homebrewed. The only beer brewed in Bratislava is Stein, although you'd never know it as Zlatý Bažant (Golden Pheasant, made by Heineken in Nitra) and Šariš (made by giants SAB Miller) are the most common taps you'll find in bars in the city. Other Slovak beers are Steiger, Tatran, Urpín, Popper, Hordan, Corgoň and Smedne Mnich (Thirsty Monk), while Topvar sponsors many local beer gardens, such as **Prešporská kúria/Pizzéria Niki** (£ @ Dunajská 21 ☎ 0910 108 107).

Beers listed as 10° (e.g. Czech Gambrinus) have less alcohol than 12° versions. Also, bear in mind that *svelte* is lager and *tmavé* is dark beer. If you fancy trying Diesel, be aware that it's a mix of light beer and coke.

See ⓦ www.kamnapivo.sk for a list (in Slovak but with icons) of some of the best beer places in town.

Once you know what to eat, there's the question of what to wash it down with. The fast answer is beer. Whether it's Czech, Slovak or German, beer is everywhere, in glasses large and small, at prices exorbitant or unbelievably low. However, the region's wine heritage is one of Bratislava's best-kept secrets, and many traditional and contemporary restaurants have a fine selection of local wines.

Traditional spirits – homemade is the best – such as *slivovica* (from plums) or *borovička* (from juniper berries) are the shots you'll be offered by new Slovak friends. They are a tad harsh, so

USEFUL DINING PHRASES

A table for two, please
Stôl pre dvoch, prosím
Stwal pre dvock, proh-seem

I'm a vegetarian
Stôl pre dvoch, prosím (Ja) som vegetarián
Stwal pre dvock, proh-seem (Yah) som veghe-tahryiaan

breakfast	**lunch**	**dinner**
raňajky	obed	večera
ranyai-kih	*obed*	*vecheh-rah*

The bill, please
Večera učet, prosím
Vecheh-rah oochet, proh-seem

I would like a beer, please
Jedno pivo, prosím
Yednoh pih-voh, proh-seem

you may want to opt for the subtler herbal tastes of Becherovka (which is Czech) or Demänovka (made in Slovakia). In the winter, everyone warms up with *svařák* (mulled wine that comes in red and white varieties) or *grog* (hot rum) together with a bag of *pečené gaštany* – roast chestnuts.

Entertainment & nightlife

The word 'Partyslava' might not trip off the tongues of today's visitors, but if Bratislavans and tourists (as well as those entrepreneurs developing more and ever varying venues for the party to spread) continue using it, then Bratislava will have acquired yet another name in its long history.

The key to Bratislava's nightlife is that it doesn't necessarily happen at night. As is infinitely noticeable, as soon as winter transforms into spring, Bratislava morphs into a sea of outdoor tables and beer gardens and, whenever the sun shines, people hit these havens and begin the day's entertainment. Similarly, in winter, the best way to beat the chill is with a little *après-ski*, even if it is strictly *avant* ...

Café bars, which usually shut around midnight, provide the warm-up party, with relaxed atmosphere and food if you haven't made reservations somewhere. The chic cocktail bars

PLAY THAT GUITAR!

The Dobro, the famous and distinctive-sounding resonator guitar, was designed in 1928 by Slovakian Ján Dopjera and his brothers. Dobro is a contraction of Dopjera Brothers and means 'good' in their native Slovak language. In recent decades, the Dobro has been used by the Eagles, Lynyrd Skynyrd and Dire Straits.

and restaurants kick off later in the evening. Clubbers and DJs converge on the hotspots and the party gets started. Legendary clubs such as **Subclub** (ⓐ Nábr arm Gen Ľsvobodu ⓣ 02 5441 1183 ⓦ www.subclub.sk), and **Cirkus Barok** (ⓐ Rázusovo nábrežie ⓣ 02 5464 2091 ⓦ www.cirkusbarok.sk) still attract the crowds with newer pretenders like **Trafo** (ⓐ Ventúrska 1 (Erdődy Palace) ⓣ 02 2092 ⓦ www.trafo.sk) fuelling a more cocktail-gargling sharp-dressed crowd.

Bratislava's venues all seem to be moulded in the arty, grandmother's den of eclecticism or the new, sleek, design spaces – with little in between. Luckily, the city is easy to traverse on foot and you can descend into any open door and decide whether or not it's for you.

There aren't many specific live music venues, but restaurants often have some folk or jazz musicians to add to the atmosphere. Bratislava is on the tour of visiting international artists, such as Keane and Oasis, who usually play **Incheba Expo** (ⓐ Viedenská cesta 3–7 ⓣ 02 6727 1111 ⓦ www.incheba.sk) or **PKO** (ⓐ Nábr arm Gen Ľsvobodu 3 ⓣ 02 5910 3101 ⓦ www.bkis.sk). To check what's on around Bratislava, visit ⓦ www.fanvbratislave.sk or ⓦ www.booom.sk (which is a clubbing what's on guide).

In 2005, the *New York Times* named Bratislava as one of its top gay destinations and while the scene isn't big, it is beautiful. Try **4 Pink's** (ⓐ Župné 3 ⓦ www.4pinks.sk) and an old favourite, **Apollon** (ⓐ Panenská 24 ⓦ www.apollon-gay-club.sk). Both websites are in English, as is ⓦ www.gay.sk.

❍ *Bratislavan street entertainer*

ON SONG

Slovakia and the Slovak National Theatre have produced some internationally acclaimed opera stars, including tenor Peter Dvorský who performed at Vienna's State Opera and La Scala before returning to Bratislava. Lucia Poppova debuted in Bratislava before popping over to Vienna, as did fellow *coloraturas* Edita Gruberová.

As low-cost airlines open up Eastern Europe to more visitors, the Great British Stag Party is descending on unsuspecting cities boasting cheap beer and good times. Although, economically, Bratislava is enjoying this, it doesn't welcome some of the behaviour groups like these can bring. As a result, the British Embassy has agreed with the government that any British national breaking a law will be deported – so be warned and behave.

Sport & relaxation

Slovaks enjoy the great outdoors when they can, due probably to the long, cold winter. That said, the cold, or snow at least, is the draw whether the slope is in the High Tatras Mountains or Bratislava's Koliba. Then there is hiking and biking, popular activities along both the banks of the Danube and Koliba (see page 98).

You can hire bikes in Bratislava but with some difficulty. An agency called Luka hires them out, but it's best to ask at the tourist office (see page 136) for contact details.

In the summer, if you need to cool down, head to Veľký Draždiak, a lake south of Petržalka. Alternatively, if you fancy some wall climbing, make for Janko Kral park.

SPECTATOR SPORTS

Ice hockey Ice hockey is the national sport of the Slovak Republic and, as such, ticket prices are low and quality of play is high. Games are usually on Tuesdays, Fridays and Sundays.
HC Slovan Bratislava ⓐ Odbojárov 9 ⓒ 02 4445 6500
ⓦ www.hcslovan.sk ⓝ Bus: 39, 53, 61, 63, 74, 78; tram: 1, 2, 4

Football The other national sport is football. Bratislava has two teams, and tickets are ridiculously cheap for local games. For international games, though, prices are quite a lot higher.
ŠK Slovan Bratislava ⓐ Viktora Tegelhoffa 4 ⓒ 02 4463 6363
ⓦ www.slovanfutbal.com ⓝ Bus: 39, 53, 61, 63, 74, 78; tram: 1, 2, 4
ŠK Inter Bratislava ⓐ Junácka 10 ⓒ 02 4445 5889
ⓦ www.interbratislava.sk ⓝ Bus: 39, 53, 61, 63, 74, 78; tram: 1, 2, 4

Horse racing If you fancy a flutter, you need to find the hippodrome for some horse racing at Petržalka. Races are usually on Sunday afternoons between April and October. **Závodisko Bratislava** ⓐ Starohájska 29 ⓣ 02 6241 1504 ⓦ www.zavodisko.sk ⓝ Bus: 198

RELAXATION

In 2008, Bratislava opened its new relaxation and leisure centre, **Relaxx** (ⓐ Einsteinova ulitsa 9 ⓣ 02 6241 4040, 0911 357 028 or 02 5249 5071 ⓦ www.relaxx.sk), where you'll find pools, spas, a gym, aerobics classes, massages and children's area.

● *Climbing the walls in the Janko Kral park*

Accommodation

Bratislava is notorious for expensive accommodation, be it peak season or not. That said, as with everything else in this burgeoning capital city, more options are becoming available. Last-minute deals can be obtained from the tourist office and usually comprise private rooms in residential houses.

HOTELS & GUEST HOUSES

Castle Club ££ Small, homely B&B on the steep path up to Bratislava Castle, with Wi-Fi. It also has numerous apartments, all central with all services and appliances included and discounts available. ⓐ Zámocké schody 4 (New Town, Bratislava Castle & the river) ⓣ 02 5464 1472 ⓦ www.stayslovakia.sk ⓝ Tram: 1, 4, 5, 9, 12, 17

Chez David ££ Small, personal service with less-than-luxurious rooms and one apartment. Location and the restaurant are the real draws. ⓐ Zámocká 13 (New Town, Bratislava Castle & the river) ⓣ 02 5441 3824 ⓦ www.chezdavid.sk ⓝ Tram: 1, 5, 9

City Hostel ££ With all en suite rooms and no dorms, this isn't a hostel except in price. New, clean and very sufficient.

> ### PRICE CATEGORIES
> Gradings are based on the approximate price of an en suite room for two people in high season, including tax.
> £ up to €35   ££ €35–135   £££ over €135

ⓐ Obchodná 38 (New Town, Bratislava Castle & the river)
ⓣ 02 5263 6041 ⓦ www.cityhostel.sk ⓝ Tram: 5, 7, 9, 13

Hotel Antares ££ Lovely converted villa in residential area
with terrace, luxurious rooms and relaxation centre. ⓐ Šulekova
15 (New Town, Bratislava Castle & the river) ⓣ 02 5464 8971
ⓦ www.hotelantares.sk ⓝ Bus: 203, 207, 208

Hotel Kyjev ££ A Communist landmark and slice of history with
little style but a big smile. ⓐ Rajská 2 (Old Town) ⓣ 02 5964 1111
ⓦ www.kyjev-hotel.sk ⓝ Bus: 202, 205; tram: 1, 4, 7, 11, 14

Hotel Matyšák ££ New hotel with large rooms, apartments
with terrace, free internet and a wine cellar with 4,000 bottles
beneath your room. Excellent. ⓐ Pražská 15 (New Town, Bratislava
Castle & the river) ⓣ 02 2063 4001 ⓦ www.hotelmatysak.sk
ⓝ Bus: 32, 34, 41, 83, 84

Hotel Spirit ££ Wacky avant-garde architecture and healing foods,
relaxation pyramid, gallery, apartments and dorm behind the
railway station. Unique yet sparse. ⓐ Vančurova 1 (New Town,
Bratislava Castle & the river) ⓣ 02 5477 7561 ⓦ www.hotelspirit.sk
ⓝ Bus: 32, 41, 44 (special bus for the disabled), 61, 74, 93;
tram: 2, 3, 8, 13

Ibis ££ You know what you're getting with an Ibis, and this is
no different to the usual identikit experience. ⓐ Zámocká 38
(New Town, Bratislava Castle & the river) ⓣ 02 5929 2000
ⓦ www.ibishotel.com ⓝ Tram: 1, 5, 9

Koliba-Expo ££ Small but perfectly formed classic Slovak wooden chalet with Heidi-inspired rooms and apartments in the mountains. A short taxi ride from the city centre but a world away from the hustle and bustle. ⓐ Kamzíkov vrch, Koliba (Devín Castle & Greater Bratislava) ⓣ 02 5477 1764 ⓦ www.koliba-expo.sk ⓝ Bus: 203

⬥ The Radisson SAS Carlton occupies a prime historic location

Old City Hotel ££ Good deal for basic, sometimes noisy, rooms in the Old Town. No lift, three floors, under 10s stay free. ⓐ Michalská 2 (Old Town) ⓣ 02 5443 0258 ⓦ www.oldcityhotel.sk

Best Western Hotel West ££–£££ Standard rooms but with rural pursuits plus pool and sauna. With a restaurant on site. ⓐ Kamzík les, Koliba (New Town, Bratislava Castle & the river) ⓣ 02 5478 8692 ⓦ www.hotel-west.sk ⓝ Bus: 203

Crowne Plaza £££ Huge hotel with all mod cons opposite the Presidential Palace plus fusion restaurant, casino, pool and gym. ⓐ Hodžovo nám 2 (New Town, Bratislava Castle & the river) ⓣ 02 5934 8111 ⓦ www.crowne-plaza.sk ⓝ Bus: 31, 34, 39, 59, 80; tram: 5, 7, 9, 13

Hotel Apollo £££ Traditional hotel with upgraded rooms and services. Worth staying for the game restaurant alone. ⓐ Dulovo nám 1 (New Town, Bratislava Castle & the river) ⓣ 02 5596 8922 ⓦ www.apollohotel.sk ⓝ Bus: 50, 68

Hotel Danube £££ Views, well-appointed rooms and a fitness centre situated aptly along the river. ⓐ Rybné nám 1 (Old Town) ⓣ 02 5934 0000 ⓦ www.bratislava.parkinn.sk ⓝ Bus: 29, 30, 37, 70, 91, 191; tram: 4, 12, 14

Hotel Devín £££ Not at Devín Castle, but with fitness centre, Wi-Fi, classically styled, fully appointed rooms in the historic centre and on the Danube. ⓐ Riečna 4 (Old Town) ⓣ 02 5443 3640 ⓦ www.hoteldevin.sk ⓝ Tram: 1, 11, 12, 14

Hotel Hradná brána £££ Enjoy a rural retreat at this new and very comfortable 11-room hotel with relax centre and restaurant. ⓐ Slovanské nábr 15, Devín (New Town, Bratislava Castle & the river) ⓣ 02 6010 2511 ⓦ www.hotelhb.sk ⓝ Bus: 29

Hotel Marrol's £££ A member of Small Luxury Hotels of the World and it is – leather furniture in the lobby, luxury in every room. ⓐ Tobrucká 4 (Old Town) ⓣ 02 5778 4600 ⓦ www.hotelmarrols.sk ⓝ Tram: 4, 11, 12, 13, 14

Hotel Perugia £££ Small and central with personalised service and an excellent Slovak restaurant. ⓐ Zelená 5 (Old Town) ⓣ 02 5443 1818 ⓦ www.perugia.sk

Radisson SAS Carlton £££ A new hotel for an historical location that cannot be bettered. Pure luxury. ⓐ Hviezdoslavovo nám 3 (Old Town) ⓣ 02 5939 0000 ⓦ www.radissonsas.com ⓝ Tram: 4, 11, 12, 13, 14

HOSTELS

Downtown Backpackers £ Popular and busy, it has character and dark corners. ⓐ Panenská 31 (New Town, Bratislava Castle & the river) ⓣ 02 5464 1191 ⓦ www.backpackers.sk ⓝ Bus: 61, 81, 93, 208

Patio Hostel £ Rooms and dorms with shared bathrooms. Cleanliness fluctuates but free internet and cool folk are a draw. Strictly no smoking. ⓐ Špitálska 35 (Old Town) ⓣ 02 5292 5797 ⓦ www.patiohostel.com ⓝ Tram: 1, 4, 7, 11, 14

THE BEST OF BRATISLAVA

Bratislava draws you in with its historic centre, imposing castle, renowned river, and buzzing cultural and night life. Then, if you stay a little longer, you discover so much more.

TOP 10 ATTRACTIONS

- **Bratislavský hrad (Bratislava Castle)** The seat of the Hungarian kings and queens and summer home of Maria Theresa, Bratislava Castle is now a wonderful museum with temporary and permanent exhibits (see page 77)

- **Hrad Devín (Devín Castle)** Border outpost of the Roman Empire and cultural heart of the Slovak nation, there has been a settlement here since 4000 BC (see page 93)

- **Kostol a kláštor františkánov (Franciscan Church and Monastery)** The city's oldest church is a drastic, fantastic, dramatic Gothic treat (see page 66)

- **Michalská brána (St Michael's Gate)** The only surviving gate of the city's medieval fortifications, the tower is now a museum and affords spectacular views of Bratislava and beyond (see page 66)

Architectural detail in the Old Town

- **Konkatedrála sv Martina (St Martin's Cathedral)**
  Bratislava's largest and most important church. Today,
  classical concerts, a crypt and skeletal remains beneath
  a glass floor draw spectators (see page 65)

- **Slovenská národná galéria (Slovak National Gallery)**
  Permanent and temporary exhibitions of Slovak and
  European art housed in the old water barracks and
  a modern annexe (see page 85)

- **The *korzo*** The name for the pedestrian section, where
  you can lose yourself in the streets, alleys and courtyards
  of Bratislava's Old Town and castle environs (see page 60)

- **Slavín Monument** Before the Soviets wrested power from
  an independent Czechoslovakia, the Red Army liberated
  the city from the Nazis in 1945. This is the monument to
  their fallen Soviet comrades (see page 100)

- **Ice hockey** The Slovaks excel at their national sport and
  were World Champions in 2002. Games are cheap and
  thrilling – whether you know the rules or not (see page 35)

- **The Danube** Wander along the river, then walk (or waltz)
  across the Danube to Janka Kráľa gardens. Don't miss
  Nový most, as if you could (see page 83)

Suggested itineraries

HALF-DAY: BRATISLAVA IN A HURRY

Wander around the historic centre and visit the Bratislava Castle grounds (for free) or take a look inside the castle itself. A walking or vintage car tour, chaffeur driven, will allow you to see the maximum amount in a limited time. Ask at the tourist office for details (see page 136).

1 DAY: TIME TO SEE A LITTLE MORE

Start your day with the above tour. Then relax in one of the city's many eateries. Wash down your lunch with a beer or glass of wine, then make your way to Devín Castle (see page 93), the historical and cultural heart of Slovakia. Alternatively, visit a museum locally – why not have a gander at the Slovak National Gallery (see page 85)?

● *Awe-inspiring Devín Castle*

BRATISLAVA CITY CARD
This discount card is available from any of the tourist
information offices (see page 136). The card allows
unlimited travel on all of Bratislava's public transport.
It also gives a free and informative walking tour of the
Old Town. Cards are available for one, two or three days.

2–3 DAYS: TIME TO SEE MUCH MORE

This amount of time will give you plenty of opportunity to
explore some of the city's palaces and museums. What's more,
you'll be able to get fully acquainted with both Bratislava and
Devín Castles (see pages 77 & 93). Both have wonderful
museums and interesting surroundings. The views around Devín
particularly are breathtaking. If you still have time, take a trip
to the Small Carpathians for some wine tasting. An encounter
with the beautiful Slovak countryside and the fabulous Červený
kameň castle will fill a whole day.

LONGER: ENJOYING BRATISLAVA TO THE FULL

With even more time on your hands, you'll really be able
to get to know the cobbled streets, parks, castle, palaces and
museums of the city. Head out and explore the surroundings,
beginning with Devín Castle. Then partake of some rural
activities on Koliba, whether it is winter or summer. A Carpathian
wine tour makes a great day out, as does a visit to Vienna or
even Budapest.

Something for nothing

Happily for visitors, Slovakia's adoption of the euro does not seem radically to have altered Bratislava's status as a city that's comparatively cheap to enjoy.

With summer festivals, concerts and activities occurring in many public spaces, finding something for nothing isn't difficult if you ever tire of just walking around Bratislava's winding streets and beautiful parks observing ornate details and quirky facts. In addition, museum entrance fees are nominal, so seeing the city's rich cultural history is within everybody's means. Museums are free on International Museum & Gallery Day (18 May). Also, the extensive grounds around Bratislava Castle are free, as is visiting the Slavín Monument and venturing to the top of the Kamzík TV Tower, both of which afford a superb vista of the city illustrating the contrast of new and old architecture.

A delightful find on the square at the Old Town end of Obchodná (ⓐ Hurbanovo nám) is a group of objects on the small lawn that appear at first glance to be a piece of wood and a manhole cover perhaps. The Dancing Bells are actually nine metal panels forming a carillon to be stepped on to produce music. They are fascinating, especially if someone actually has some musical talent. Check out the wobbly bench, too.

The huge outdoor **Miletičova market** (ⓛ Mon–Sat ⓝ Tram: 8, 9, 14 to Záhradnícka) is a great place to see the real Bratislava. You can find fresh produce grown by the sellers themselves, home-pickled foodstuffs, arts and crafts, plus clothes and objects you might never have thought to find at a market. It is free to browse and cheap if you decide to buy something.

● *There are plenty of free festivals and concerts around the city*

When it rains

Rain isn't necessarily the reason you'll want to head inside while touring Bratislava: plummeting temperatures and horizontal sleet are often a deciding factor for winter visitors. By far the most accessible retreat in times of adverse weather conditions is the nearest cosy bar or café. Hot chocolate, mulled wine or a beer will brighten any day and one of the beauties of Bratislava is that no matter where you are when the heavens open, you're never far from a bar/café of some version.

Another obvious refuge is a museum or gallery, picking one of the larger ones to extend your shelter time. The National Gallery is sufficiently rich in beguiling rooms and corridors to warrant an extended visit that will not only fill but enrich any dreary afternoon. Another option is the **vintage car tour**, where you can sit in comfort and have a chauffeured trip round the city (🅣 0903 302 817 🅦 www.presporacik.sk 🅛 Apr–Oct only). It's only 30 minutes long, but perfect for an April shower.

If you've seen enough culture, you can always head out to shop till you drop at one of the modern malls where non-shopaholics have options too. Try bowling, or immerse yourself in an alternate reality by taking in a movie. The mall multiplexes show all the usual Hollywood blockbusters so check the schedules at **Aupark** (🅦 www.palacecinemas.sk) and **Polus** (🅦 www.istropoliscinemacenter.sk). Note that kids' movies are usually dubbed. The central **Kino Mladošt** (🅐 Hviezdoslavovo nám 17 🅣 02 5443 5000) shows quality European films, which means subtitles will only be in the Slovak language. **FK Charlie** (🅐 Špitálska 4 🅣 02 5296 8994 🅦 www.istropoliscinema.sk)

hosts quality films and festivals such as the notable One World/Jeden Svet.

⬤ *Behind the modern façade of the National Gallery lie interesting art exhibits*

On arrival

TIME DIFFERENCE
Slovakia follows Central European Time (CET), an hour ahead of Greenwich Mean Time (GMT). From late March to late October the clocks are put ahead one hour.

ARRIVING
By air
Domestic and international flights use Bratislava's **M R Štefánik airport** (ⓐ Ivánska cesta ❶ 02 3303 3353/4857 3353 ⓦ www.airportbratislava.sk), which lies 9 km (5½ miles) northeast of the city. The airport currently has three terminals: Terminal A for departures and Terminals B and C for arrivals.

Taxis are renowned for overcharging, so arrange a price first or make sure you have a reputable driver. Savvy travellers often pick up taxis from the departure terminal, where drivers have already made the trip out and might not be as keen to rip visitors off. The journey into the city centre should take between 15 and 25 minutes.

Bus 61 runs from the airport to Hlavná stanica (central train station) every 10–20 minutes from 04.45–23.45 (last bus 23.05 from the train station). There you can change onto another bus or trolleybus to take you into the city centre.

By rail
Bratislava Hlavná stanica (Central train station ⓐ Predstaničné nám 1 ⓦ www.zsr.sk/www.slovakrail.sk) provides connections around Slovakia and to and from various neighbouring countries. The train station is well linked by public transport into the city.

By road

Autobusova stanica (Bratislava's coach station ➋ Mlynské
Nivy ➊ 0972 222 222) is linked to the city centre via trolleybus.
Numbers 202, 205 and 208 are the most commonly used. Good
bus and coach links from here connect with all of Slovakia and
neighbouring countries.

With trams, buses and trolleybuses, pedestrianised zones
and Bratislava's infamous traffic jams, driving here especially
at peak times is a nightmare for the uninitiated. Car parks
are common and prices not too high. Some hotels provide
parking spaces.

FINDING YOUR FEET

Although it uses the same alphabet as English, the Slovak
language is tricky for foreign tongues to get around, so asking
for directions can be a chore. Bratislava remains a fairly parochial
city despite the ongoing developments and some Bratislavans
can seem cold and unfriendly people. These days, though, you'll
find more locals speaking English and the older generations will
always try German or merely point.

ORIENTATION

The Old Town and some connecting streets are pedestrianised,
and walking around (probably in circles for a while at least) is
the best way for orientation. Bratislava Castle is an excellent
landmark, as is the Dunaj (River Danube) itself. Tram lines
closest to the Old Town stop at Kapucínska and Kamenné
nám (Tesco). For trolleybuses, Hodžovo nám (the Presidential
Palace) and Rajská (Tesco again) are the central stops.

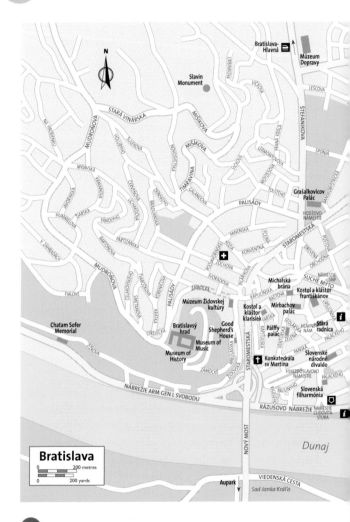

Bratislava-Hlavná

Múzeum Dopravy

Slavin Monument

STARÁ VINÁRSKA

N

Grašalkovicov Palác

PALISÁDY

STAROMESTSKÁ

Michalská brána

Kostol a kláštor františkánov

SUCHÉ MYTO

Múzeum Židovskej kultúry

Kostol a kláštor klarisiek

Mirbachov palác

Stará radnica

Chatam Sofer Memorial

Bratislavský hrad

Good Shepherd's House

Pálffy palác

Slovenské národné divaldo

Museum of Music

Museum of History

Konkatedrála sv Martina

Slovenská filharmónia

RÁZUSOVO NÁBREŽIE

NÁBREŽIE ARM GEN L SVOBODU

Dunaj

Bratislava

0   200 metres

0   200 yards

Aupark

VIEDENSKÁ CESTA

Sad Janka Kráľa

NOVÝ MOST

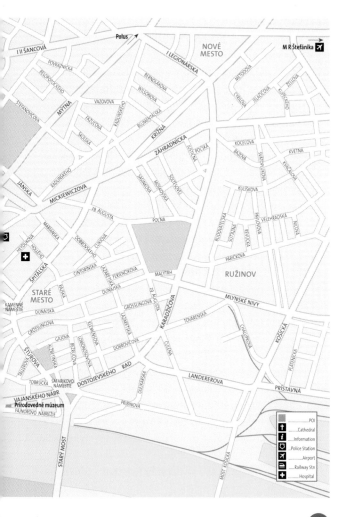

GETTING AROUND

The easiest way around is on foot, as Bratislava isn't very big. Once away from the hilly castle section, it remains fairly flat and of course a large portion is dedicated to pedestrians. For the Old Town, it's walking only, as public transport runs a ring around these small, winding and often cobbled streets. If you have a hotel in the Old Town, taxis might drop you at the door.

There are 13 tram lines, 15 trolleybuses (which are trackless trams) and 69 bus lines. Some 20 night bus routes run from 23.30 to 03.30. A superb website (ⓦ www.imhd.sk) lists all routes and times, and is in English. The main interchanges are Hodžovo nám, Nový most and Kamenné nám. As Bratislava's entire transport system is integrated, one ticket will cover all forms of transport. That said, you must buy tickets before getting on board. You'll get these from a ticket shop (at the bus and train stations, for example), *tabak* kiosk or yellow vending machine. Additionally, you must validate the ticket by inserting it in the orange or red franking machines by the doors of trams and buses. If a tram or trolleybus door doesn't open, push the button above the doors.

Tickets cost €0.50 for a 15-minute journey and €0.70 for 60 minutes. Reduced fares for the tickets are €0.25 and €0.35 respectively. A 24-hour ticket costs €3.50, a 48-hour ticket costs €6.50, a three-day ticket costs €8 and a week's ticket is €12. These are worth getting, as they'll pay the way to Devín Castle, for example.

What's more, if you have no ticket or one that's not validated, you face a fine.

IF YOU GET LOST, TRY ...

Do you speak English?
Hovoríte po anglicky?
Hovoh-ree-tyeh poh ahnglits-kih?

How do I get to ...?
Ako sa dostanem do ...?
Akoh sa dostah-nyem doh ...?

Where's ...?
Kde je ...?
Gdyeh yeh ...?

Can you show me (on the map)?
Môžete mi ukázat' (na mape)?
Muo-zhetyeh mih uh-kaazaty (nah mapeh)?

Make sure the ticket inspector shows his credentials before you start paying out and don't forget public transport is free with the Bratislava City Card (see page 45). On public holidays, the Sunday timetable operates.

As usual, be careful when hailing a passing taxi – unless you know how much your journey should cost. Company names, rather than an unmarked car with a yellow taxi light, are safer and cheaper. Hotel taxis are more expensive. Do not hesitate to ask the restaurant or venue you are at to call a taxi for you. Alternatively, try these:
MB Taxi ✆ 02 16916 or 0902 916 916 (mobile)
Super Taxi ✆ 02 16616 or 0903 616 616 (mobile)

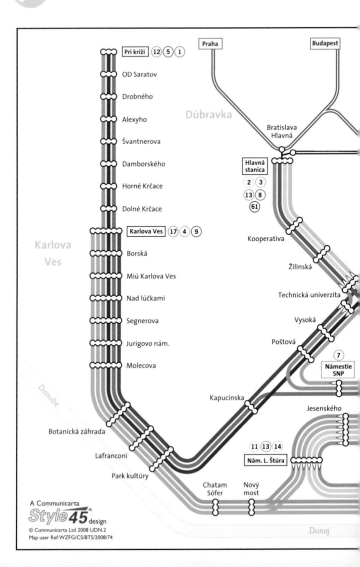

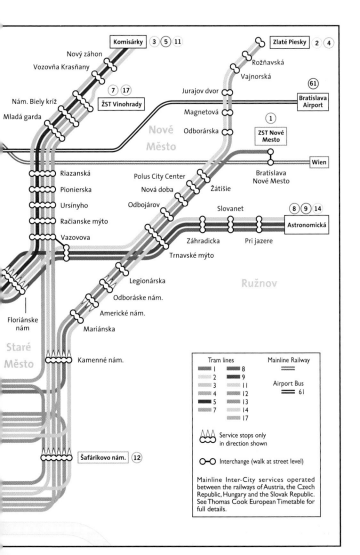

DANUBE CRUISE

Bratislava sits prettily on the Danube between Budapest and Vienna, both of which have river connections. You can also journey up and down the Danube on a shorter sightseeing tour or a dinner cruise. The Danube does have low water problems, which could postpone or even cancel your trip. Cruises cease in winter.

LOD ⓐ Fajnorovo nábrežie 2 ❶ 02 5293 2226 ⓦ www.lod.sk
Twin City Liner ⓐ Rázusovo nábrežie ⓦ www.twincityliner.com

CAR HIRE

A car is extremely useful for excursions around Bratislava, although there may be some arguments on the designated driver for touring the wine region. However, if you are staying in the city for sightseeing, park the car and wander on foot.

Booking a hire car with your plane ticket often saves money, although firms have offices in Bratislava, too. You'll find the following in the arrivals hall:

Avis ❶ 02 4341 0709 ⓦ www.avis.sk
Eurocar ❶ 02 4319 1474 ⓦ www.eurocar.sk
Hertz ❶ 02 5720 1261 ⓦ www.hertz.sk
Sixt ❶ 02 4333 6609 ⓦ www.sixt.sk

● *Ancient and modern – a view over the Bratislava rooftops*

THE CITY OF
Bratislava

Old Town

The winding streets of Bratislava's Old Town are a walk into history, with beautiful buildings featuring commemoration plaques to such luminaries as Mozart, Liszt and Pálffy. The lanes meander around the central areas of Hlavné námestie (Main Square), and Hviezdoslavovo námestie, and are bordered by Staromestká street leading to Nový most (New Bridge) towards the castle, Michalská brána (St Michael's Gate) towards Obchodná street, Námestie SNP, Štúrova street and, of course, the Danube. The *korzo* (as the area is known) has no public transport – except trams passing by the National Theatre – but it is small and perfect to explore for hours on foot, especially the not-yet-renovated area around Prepoštská and Kapitulská streets.

SIGHTS & ATTRACTIONS

Hlavné námestie (Main Square)

The main square was and is the hub of life in the city. In the past, this area was used as the main market (check out the yard sticks and butcher's knife on the left of the entrance to the Old Town Hall), as well as for executions and celebrations.

The fountain at the heart of the square was commissioned by Maximilian II in 1572 after fire swept through the square. It is known as the Maximilian Fountain, or the Roland Fountain as Max is depicted in full knight's armour à la Roland.

It is said that, on New Year's Eve, Roland will turn around and even walk! But we have yet to see it, as there are conditions

◎ *Explore the alleyways of the Old Town*

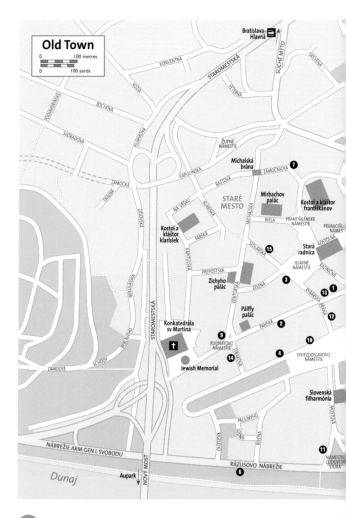

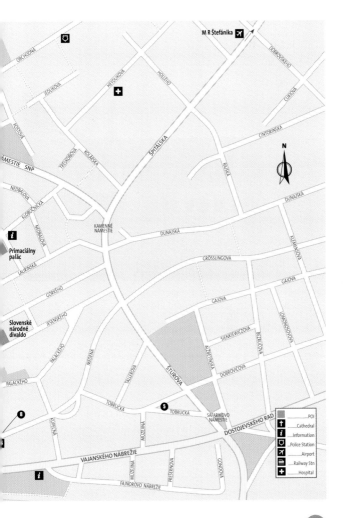

● *Hlavné námestie, the focal point of the Old Town*

attached to the miracle that have precluded its occurrence – one is that a sober, Bratislavan-born virgin be present.

Hviezdoslavovo námestie (Hviezdoslav's Square)

The largest city square was the location of the moat filled in by Maria Theresa to allow for extensive construction when the city walls were torn down. It is lined with restaurants, cafés and bars, has a free ice rink in the winter, a giant chessboard in summer, saw George W Bush address the nation, is home to the German and US Embassies, the National Theatre and Philharmonic buildings, and it hosts the Christmas market.

Jewish Memorial

The Jewish quarter and beautiful synagogue were demolished in 1969 to make way for Nový most, which didn't endear the modern bridge to the people. The etching of the synagogue on smooth marble appears to have restored its location as it merges with adjacent buildings' reflections. The Holocaust monument says on it 'Remember' in both Slovakian and Hebrew. Hannukah and other holidays continue to be celebrated here. ⓐ Rudnayovo nám

Konkatedrála sv Martina (St Martin's Cathedral)

St Martin's Cathedral is the largest and most important of Bratislava's church buildings: Pope John Paul II celebrated and

BRATISLAVA'S STATUES

Hans Christian Andersen (ⓐ Hviezdoslavovo nám, opposite the US Embassy) travelled through Bratislava in 1840 and this statue of the master storyteller illustrates his imagination. Unfortunately, someone stole the cute ugly duckling from his feet, but the sculptor has promised a replacement.

The top-hatted **Schöner Naci statue** (ⓐ Rybárska brána) is of Ignac Lamar, a local dandy who, denied his one true love, wandered the city giving flowers to women and sweets to children until his death in 1967. He too was vandalised – by a British stag party – and is now watched over by CCTV.

Liszt conducted mass here. Construction began in 1221, but it wasn't consecrated until 1452 due to wars and lack of funds. Between 1563 and 1830, its hallowed halls saw 19 Hungarian kings and queens crowned, and the 300 g (10 oz) gilt crown atop its 85 m (279 ft) tall tower is a replica of their crown. Its Gothic interior holds four chapels, a crypt (take a torch), and a spectacular statue by Juraj Raphael Donner depicting St Martin.

The cathedral was built into the city walls. You can see a remaining section opposite the entrance, and this placement made it impossible to have the entrance facing the altar as is usual. Concerts are regularly held here and although you cannot hear the rumblings from the busy road, you can feel them.
ⓐ Rudnayovo nám ⓛ 09.00–11.30, 13.00–17.00 Mon–Sat, 13.30–16.00 Sun, Apr–Oct; 09.00–11.30, 13.00–16.00 Mon–Sat, 13.30–16.00 Sun, Nov–Mar

Kostol a kláštor františkánov (Franciscan Church and Monastery)
The Franciscan church and monastery is a fabulous Gothic building completed in 1297, making it the oldest church in the city. It was also the final stop on the coronation route from the castle. Political shenanigans have been held here over the centuries.
ⓐ Františkánske nám ⓛ English-language Mass: 09.00, 19.30 Mon–Sat, 10.30, 12.00, 16.30, 18.30 Sun

Michalská brána (St Michael's Gate)
St Michael's is the only surviving gate from the medieval fortification of the city. The 51 m (167 ft) tower holds the fascinating Museum of Arms and City Fortifications on six floors and affords a magnificent view from the top. ⓐ Michalská 22

🔺 *The view from Michalská brána (St Michael's Gate)*

🕐 02 5443 3044 🕐 10.00–17.00 Tues–Fri, 11.00–18.00 Sat & Sun.
Admission charge

Mirbachov palác (Mirbach Palace)

Mirbach is a beautiful rococo palace built between 1768 and
1770 and today is home to the City Gallery of Bratislava, with
temporary and permanent exhibits of mostly baroque artists.
ⓐ Františkánske nám 11 🕐 02 5443 1556 🔘 www.gmb.sk
🕐 11.00–18.00. Admission charge

Pálffy palác (Pálffy Palace)

Pálffy Palace was discovered to have a Gothic origin during

reconstruction, and Celtic and Roman finds were also uncovered. The City Gallery of Bratislava holds temporary and permanent exhibits here. A plaque on the wall in the part that is now the Austrian Embassy commemorates Mozart's concert in 1762 at the age of six. ⓐ Panská 19 ⓣ 02 5443 3627 ⓦ www.gmb.sk ⓛ 11.00–18.00. Admission charge

Primaciálny palác (Primate's Palace)

The pink neoclassical Primate's Palace was built between 1778 and 1781, and holds some of the world's most precious tapestries (made by royal decree in England for Charles I in the 17th century), which depict the doomed love of Hero and Leander. The building is also famous for a 150 kg (330 lb) iron cardinal's hat atop its pediment and, in 1805 following the Battle of Austerlitz, the Peace of Pressburg was signed here between France and Austria. The pediment is decorated with a mosaic comprising 3,200 coloured pebbles from the Danube. The interior courtyard sports a statue of St George (Slovakia's patron saint) slaying his dragon. ⓐ Primaciálne námesti 3 ⓣ 02 5935 6394 ⓦ www.gmb.sk ⓛ 10.00–17.00. Admission charge

Stará radnica (Old Town Hall)

Bratislava's Old Town Hall stands testament to its age with three architectural styles incorporated over five centuries. Gothic benches from the 14th century sit next to the 15th-century house and tower built by the first mayor, Jakub, who donated the house to the city when he was elected for the first (of 35) times.

The fabulous Museum of Feudal Justice is the oldest in the city and dates back to 1868; it features archaeological

◗ The various architectural styles of the Stará radnica (Old Town Hall)

objects from the Stone Age to the 1950s, via pots, coins, jewels, swords, paintings and so on. The stairs are steep and spiral, the torture pits and instruments are in the basement, and the retro-manic exhibit on Slovak life in the mid-20th century is superb. Both Town Hall and Museum are closed until 2010 for renovation. ⓐ Primaciálne námetsie 3 ⓣ 02 5920 5130 ⓦ www.muzeum.bratislava.sk

CULTURE

Slovenská filharmónia (Slovakian Philharmonic)
The beautiful Philharmonic building has rented out part of its premises to Reduta restaurant and casino, but musical performances occur here regularly. ⓐ Palackého ⓣ 02 5920 8218 or 5920 8292 ⓦ www.filharm.sk ⓛ 13.00–19.00 Mon & Tues, Thur & Fri, 08.00–14.00 Wed

Slovenské národné divadlo (Slovak National Theatre)
The Slovak National Theatre, home to Bratislava's opera and ballet performances, was built in 1886 to designs by the alliterative architects Ferdinand Fellner and Herman Helmer. The fountain, depicting Zeus as an eagle carrying Ganymede off to be the gods' cup bearer, is the work of Viktor Tilgner and was placed here in 1888. Inside is no less spectacular with more than 2,000 lights illuminating its renowned performances. In 2008, an annexe to the main building opened at Pribinova 17. ⓐ Hviezdoslavovo nám ⓦ www.snd.sk. Tickets can be obtained from the box office ⓐ Hviezdoslavovo nám ⓣ 02 544 31 723 ⓦ www.ticketportal.sk ⓛ 12.00–17.30 Mon–Fri

CORONATION PATH
The golden crowns in the streets identify the route that
was followed by the coronation procession. The route
starts at St Martin's and continues along Kapitulská,
Prepoštská, Ventúrska and Sedlárska streets to Hlavné
námestie. City representatives greeted the king in front
of the Old Town Hall, and he then continued to
Františkánske námestie.

Zichyho palác (Zichyho Palace)
Lovely courtyard and house used as a concert venue and
gallery. ⓐ Ventúrska 9 ① 0903 468 776 Ⓦ www.galeria-z.sk
🕓 12.00–18.00 Mon–Sat

RETAIL THERAPY

Folk Art Traditional woodwork and ceramics plus clothing
and toys. ⓐ Panská 2 ① 02 5443 4874 🕓 10.00–18.00 Mon–Fri,
10.00–14.00 Sat

Stará Tržnica An old covered market selling fruit and veg, and
with some exceedingly cheap lunch options. ⓐ Nám SNP 25
🕓 06.00–00.00

Vinotéka Sv Urbana Local wines at very competitive prices.
ⓐ Klobučnícka 4 ① 02 5443 2537 Ⓦ www.vinotekasvurbana.sk
🕓 10.00–18.00 Mon–Fri, 10.00–14.00 Sat

TAKING A BREAK

Čajovňa Pohoda £ ❶ Take it easy and get healthy in this Zen tea room decked out with cool tables, mosaics, chess and dominoes, etc. ❷ Laurinská 3 ❸ 02 5443 3103 ❹ 10.30–23.00 Mon–Fri, 12.00–23.00 Sat & Sun

🔺 *The quirky statue of Ignac Lamar*

Gatto Matto £ ❷ Delicious cheap eats, English papers and magazines plus free internet in the courtyard of the British Council. Oh, and strictly no smoking. ⓐ Panská 17 ⓣ 02 5443 8408 ⓦ www.gattomatto.sk ⓛ 10.00–22.00 Mon–Fri, 11.00–22.00 Sat

Schokocafe Maximilian £ ❸ In the supposedly haunted House of the Black Lady, savour the aroma and taste of all things chocolate, including a fountain. But no smoking, please. ⓐ Hlavné nám 3 ⓣ 02 5441 0196 ⓛ 08.00–22.00

Verne Café £ ❹ A good mix of locals and expats in this arty den of a café, which serves up booze, coffee, food and atmosphere to the sound of chill tunes. ⓐ Hviezdoslavovo nám 18 ⓣ 02 5443 0514 ⓛ 08.30–00.00 Mon–Thur, 08.30–01.00 Fri, 10.00–01.00 Sat, 11.00–00.00 Sun

AFTER DARK

RESTAURANTS
Pizza Mizza £ ❺ In the Old Town but with a distinctly neighbourhood feel and great oven-cooked pizza. ⓐ Tobrucká 5 ⓣ 02 5296 5034 ⓦ www.pizzamizza.sk ⓛ 10.00–23.00 Mon–Fri, 11.00–23.00 Sat & Sun

Botel Gracia ££ ❻ Fabulous views from this floating hotel restaurant and terrace served with good international and grill dishes. ⓐ Rázusovo nábr ⓣ 02 5443 2132 ⓦ www.botelgracia.sk ⓛ 07.00–22.00

Prašná Bašta ££ ❼ Famous cellar space with garden serving huge portions of local cuisine, accompanied by traditional live music. ⓐ Zámočnícka 11 ⓣ 02 5443 4957 ⓦ www.prasnabasta.sk ⓛ 11.00–23.00

Reštaurácia Reduta ££ ❽ Fabulous dining under the vaulted ceilings of the Philharmonic building. ⓐ Medená 3 ⓣ 02 5443 5242 ⓦ www.reduta.sk ⓛ 11.00–23.00 Mon–Sat

Camouflage £££ ❾ Cool design and fabulous food in Erdödy Palace (plus adjacent café, Flowers restaurant and club). ⓐ Ventúrska 1 ⓣ 02 2092 2711 ⓦ www.camouflage.sk ⓛ 11.30–01.00 Mon–Sat

Kogo £££ ❿ Superb Italian restaurant originally from Prague, with a relaxed atmosphere. ⓐ Hviezdoslavovo nám 21 ⓣ 02 5464 5094 ⓦ www.kogo.sk ⓛ 08.00–23.00

Malecón £££ ⓫ The glitterati flock here for the impressive interior, cuisine, superbly mixed cocktails and to mix with other folk whose chauffeurs are waiting outside. ⓐ Nám Ľudovíta Štúra ⓣ 0910 274 583 ⓦ www.malecon.sk ⓛ 11.00–01.00 Mon–Wed, 11.00–03.00 Thur–Sat, 11.00–23.00 Sun

Mezzo Mezzo £££ ⓬ The late kitchen draws the post-theatre crowd to savour international cuisine with an Asian bent. ⓐ Rybárska brána 9 ⓣ 02 5443 4393 ⓦ www.mezzo.sk ⓛ 08.00–01.00 Mon–Fri, 09.00–01.00 Sat & Sun

Paparazzi £££ ⑬ Sophisticated space with quality Italian cuisine, fine wines and cosmopolitan atmosphere in its dark, warm wood interior divided well for privacy. ⓐ Laurínska 1 ⓣ 02 5464 7971 ⓦ www.paparazzi.sk ⓛ 10.00–01.00

Sushi Bar Tokyo £££ ⑭ Unremarkable ambience in this restaurant but the courtyard terrace, succulent sushi and spicy Thai make it worthwhile. ⓐ Strakova 2 ⓣ 02 5443 4982 ⓦ www.sushi-bar.sk ⓛ 11.00–00.00

Tempus Fugit £££ ⑮ A classy restaurant in a beautifully restored 15th-century building with covered courtyard and romantic balconies. ⓐ Sedlárska 5 ⓣ 02 5441 4357 ⓦ www.tempusfugit.sk ⓛ 10.00–01.00

BARS

17's Bar A somewhat seedy bar well loved for its simple food, good beer (e.g. Hoegaarden) and ambience. ⓐ Hviezdoslavovo nám 17 ⓣ 02 5443 5135 ⓦ www.17bar.sk ⓛ 10.00–00.00 Mon–Wed, 10.00–01.00 Thur, 10.00–02.00 Fri & Sat, 10.00 – 23.00 Sun

Café de Zwaan Belgium in Bratislava with 13 beers, including Leffe and Hoegaarden on tap, plus bowls of steaming mussels all served by efficient and friendly staff. What more do you want? ⓐ Panská 7 ⓣ 02 5441 9166 ⓦ www.dezwaan.sk ⓛ 11.00–01.00

The Dubliner The Irish pub overseas: full of stag parties, sports fans and the occasional girl. Unsophisticated fun. ⓐ Sedlárska 6

🕿 02 5441 0706 Ⓦ www.irish-pub.sk 🕒 11.00–03.00 Mon–Sat, 11.00–01.00 Sun

Greenwich Cocktails and coffee for a suited and booted crowd oozing after-work sex appeal till way past the mean time. Ⓐ Zelená 10 🕿 0910 760 222 Ⓦ www.greenwich.sk 🕒 16.00–02.00

Hacienda Mexicana & El Diablo The usual cheesy Tex-Mex décor and cuisine entice a lively, young crowd to eat then party like there's no *mañana*. Ⓐ Sedlárska 6 🕿 0904 556 886 Ⓦ www.mexicana.sk 🕒 08.30–02.30 Mon–Sat, 10.30–00.30 Sun

K Bar Sheet music papers the walls and you are the star in this karaoke bar, when the barman isn't doing his adrenalin-fuelled cocktail show. Ⓐ Zelená 8 🕿 0905 621 508 🕒 11.00–06.00 Mon–Sat, 12.00–06.00 Sun

Prazdroj A Czech pub, with copper fermentation vats, serving Czech favourites Plzeňský Prazdroj (that's Pilsner Urquell) and Kozel along with the hearty food to sop up the brew. Ⓐ Mostová 8 🕿 02 5441 1108 🕒 10.00–00.00 Mon, 10.00–01.00 Tues–Thur, 10.00–02.00 Fri, 11.00–02.00 Sat, 11.00–00.00 Sun

Slang Pub A drinking den that manages to attract locals and tourists alike for great food and ambience around its sprawling rooms and long bar. Ⓐ Hviezdoslavovo nám 23 🕿 02 5443 5073 Ⓦ www.slangpub.host.sk 🕒 10.00–00.00 Sun & Mon, 10.00–01.00 Tues–Thur, 10.00–02.00 Fri & Sat

New Town, Bratislava Castle & the river

Surrounding the Old Town proper are ever greater glories to Bratislava's past – including the royal seat, Bratislava Castle. The streets aren't all as narrow and picturesque as the Old Town, but the cobbled lanes outside the city walls leading to the castle are full of character and hidden gems. Away from the cultural part of town, too, you'll find lovely parks, malls and a more local side of Bratislava nightlife.

SIGHTS & ATTRACTIONS

Bratislavský hrad (Bratislava Castle)

The imposing (although it is also known as 'the upside-down table') Bratislava Castle sits on its fortifications looking down on its city. The Slovakian Parliament is located next door – there is a tunnel leading from Parliament to the castle. Some rooms are used today for official government functions (Putin and Bush met here in 2005) but on the whole, the castle is now a museum, which is closed for renovation until 2011.

This strategic site was first settled in the Bronze Age, but it was after the Hungarian defeat at the hands of the Turks in 1526 that their empire's capital was moved from the now-occupied Buda to Bratislava, or Pressburg as it was called then. In 1563, Maximilian II, son of Ferdinand I, was the first Hungarian monarch to be crowned in St Martin's Cathedral. The castle was rebuilt as the royal residence, the crown jewels were stored in the castle's Crown Tower (a replica is on show today) and Bratislava's importance grew. Empress Maria Theresa decreed the castle her summer residence and had it rebuilt as the residence of her favourite daughter, Maria Kristina. Under Josef II the castle was used as a seminary, and from 1802 was used to house troops. In 1811 the castle burned to the ground and remained ruined until 1953 when restoration works, which are ongoing, began.

The grand view takes in the Communist residential creation Petralžka (the industrial area of the city), and large tracts of Austria and Hungary. The museum may be closed, but it's great to admire from without and the grounds and underground well in the courtyard are free to explore.

Exploring the winding but steep streets (Zámocké or Soferove schody and Beblavého) leading up to the castle is part of the experience, but if you've walked enough, then hop on buses 203 or 207.

Grounds ⏰ 08.00–21.30 May–Sept; 09.00–18.00 Oct–Apr

Domček u Dobreho pastiera (Good Shepherd's House)

This narrow, single-room-span building is a magnificent example of a rococo *burgher* (citizen) house. Having been built in 1760, luckily it wasn't destroyed in the 1960s. Narrow, steep stairs (check out the guy cables keeping house and home together) lead to three rather shabby floors of exhibits of the Museum of Historic Clocks – including tools, pictures of clocks, pictures with working clocks in them and clocks themselves.

ⓐ Židovská 1 ☎ 02 5441 1940 ⓦ www.muzeum.bratislava.sk
⏰ 10.00–17.00 Thur & Fri, 11.00–18.00 Sat & Sun.
Admission charge

⬥ *Bratislavský hrad (Bratislava Castle) dominates the city*

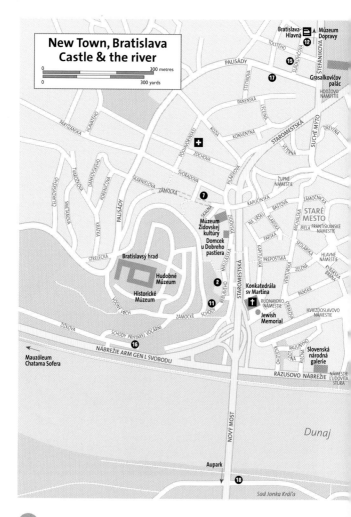

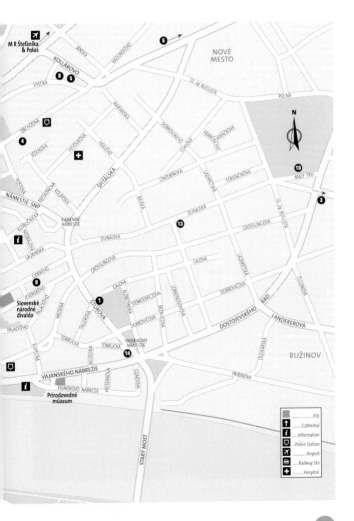

Grasalkovičov palác (Grasalkovič Palace)

Today's Presidential Palace was built as the summer home of Count Anton Grasalkovič (1695–1771) in 1760 when Maria Theresa's visits made it the centre of high society. The palace first became the residence of the President of the Slovak Republic in the 1940s. The interior includes superb frescoes and a unique staircase. It isn't open to the public but the manicured gardens are. ⓐ Hodžovo nám ⓦ www.prezident.sk ◷ Park: 08.00–22.00 June–Sept; 10.00–20.00 Apr–May; 10.00–19.00 Oct–Mar

Old city wall from Good Shepherd's House

Mauzóleum Chatama Sofera (Chatam Sofer Memorial)

The recently created Chatam Sofer Memorial is a moving reminder of Bratislava's Jewish community. In 1806, Chatam Sofer, born Moshe Schreiber in 1762, became Chief Rabbi of Bratislava, where he lived and worked till his death in 1839. The memorial has an underground chamber containing 23 graves (including Chatam Sofer's), plus 41 tombstones that escaped destruction of the Jewish cemetery. The glass represents the gravestones that were destroyed. Call in advance to enter. ⓐ Nábr Arm Gen L'Svobodu ① 0903 821 432 Ⓦ www.chatamsofer.com ① 14.00–16.00 Sun–Fri Ⓝ Tram: 4, 12, 17

Nový most (New Bridge)

The asymmetrical cable-stayed bridge dominates every view of the city – unless you are on it. The New Bridge was opened in 1972 and has always been known as the UFO Bridge for its flying saucer-like restaurant atop its supporting pillars on the Petržalka side. Indeed, the restaurant is now called UFO. There are 430 steps in the right leg, but the left leg holds a lift that'll whisk you up to the view of views. The bridge has lanes for cars, bikes and pedestrians. ① 02 6252 0300 Ⓦ www.u-f-o.sk ① 10.00–23.00. Admission charge to both legs, unless you have a reservation at the restaurant

Sad Janka Kráľa (Janko Kral's Park)

This park, one of the oldest in Europe, was created in 1775 by Maria Theresa and is named after the Slovak poet Jan Kral. Today it is not as large as it once was, as the state built the residential high rise *panelaks* in Petržalka. Restaurant Leberfinger makes a delicious stop in the park and has a terrace, kids' play area and wine cellar. @ Tyršovo nábrežie

Restaurant Leberfinger ££ @ Viedenská cesta 257 ☏ 02 6231 7590 @ www.leberfinger.sk ⏰ 11.00–00.00

CULTURE

Historické Múzeum (Museum of History)

Objects illustrate the development of Slovakian society from the Middle Ages to the present day with representative exhibits of furniture, arts, clocks, weapons, ceramics, silver and clothing. The Crown Tower is quite a trek but affords spectacular views. This museum is part of the Bratislava Castle complex and is closed for renovation until 2011. @ Bratislavský hrad ☏ 02 5441 1444 @ www.snm.sk

Hudobné Múzeum (Museum of Music)

A fine collection of instruments documents Slovakia's rich musical heritage. There is also a recital room with an organ and another annexe in the Luginsland Bastion. This museum is part of the Bratislava Castle complex and is closed for renovation until 2011. @ Bratislavský hrad ☏ 02 5441 1444 @ www.snm.sk

Múzeum Dopravy (Transport Museum)

The Transport Museum, beautifully housed in Bratislava's first steam railway station, features a selection of carriages, engines, vehicles, equipment and more. @ Šancova 1/A ☏ 02 5244 4163

ⓦ www.muzeumdopravy.com ⓛ 10.00–17.00 Tues–Sun ⓝ Bus: 210; tram: 1, 2, 3, 8

Múzeum Židovskej kultúry (Museum of Jewish Culture)

The Museum of Jewish Culture exhibits a moving collection of artistic, religious and domestic objects from all over the country. It also documents the Holocaust and demolition of Bratislava's Jewish quarter in the 1960s. ⓐ Židovská 17 ⓣ 02 5441 8507 ⓦ www.slovak-jewish-heritage.org ⓛ 11.00–17.00 Sun–Fri. Admission charge

Prírodovedné múzeum (Natural History Museum)

The fascinating Natural History Museum holds some 2.4 million objects. Get your rocks off on four floors of permanent and temporary exhibitions. ⓐ Vajanského nábr 2 ⓣ 02 5934 9127 ⓦ www.snm.sk ⓛ 09.00–18.00 Tues–Sun, May & June; 10.00–18.00 Tues–Sun, July & Aug. Admission charge

Slovenská národná galéria (Slovak National Gallery)

The National Gallery has two entrances and two distinct buildings. The excellent well-lit new wing for temporary exhibitions has a small entrance on Mostová. A walkway links it with the Water Barracks, behind the brutal riverside façade, which holds the permanent exhibitions. ⓐ Rázusovo nábr 2 ⓣ 02 5443 2081 ⓦ www.sng.sk ⓛ 10.00–17.30 Tues–Sun. Admission charge

RETAIL THERAPY

Aupark A sizeable mall and entertainment complex offering a wide selection of shops and amenities. ⓐ Einsteinova 18, off Nový Most bridge ⓣ 02 6826 6111 ⓦ www.aupark.sk ⓛ 09.00–18.00 Mon–Sat ⓝ Bus: 50

Polus Bratislava's first ever mall! ⓐ Vajnorská 100, off Staromestká, south of Starý Most ⓣ 02 4444 1234 ⓦ www.poluscitycenter.sk ⓛ 09.00–21.00 ⓝ Bus: 50, 51, 198; tram: 1, 2, 4

ÚĽUV Financed by the Ministry of Culture and involved in the design, development and production of Slovak art and craft. Workshops on site. ⓐ Obchodná 64 ⓣ 02 5273 1349 ⓦ www.uluv.sk ⓛ 10.00–18.00 Mon–Fri, 10.00–14.00 Sat ⓝ Tram: 1, 5, 6, 7, 9

TAKING A BREAK

Bagel & Coffee Story £ ❶ Good breakfast bagels, cakes, wraps, juice and fair trade coffee. ⓐ Štúrova 13 ⓣ 02 5263 1655 ⓦ www.bagelcoffeestory.com ⓛ 07.00–20.00 Mon–Fri, 10.00–15.00 Sat & Sun ⓝ Tram: 4, 11, 12, 13, 14, 17

U Čerta £ ❷ Devilish art and ambience in this boozy, friendly, full of old furniture spot. Bar food, armchairs and chess to make you feel right at home. ⓐ Beblavého 2 ⓛ 13.00–00.00 Mon–Fri, 14.00–00.00 Sat & Sun ⓝ Tram: 1, 4, 5, 9, 12, 17

Film Café £ ❸ Chilled-out first-floor café with good drinks and food but poor choice of beer, Černá Hora. ⓐ Prievozská 18 ⓣ 0903 686 707 ⓛ 10.00–00.00 Mon–Thur, 10.00–01.00 Fri & Sat, 12.00–00.00 Sun ⓝ Bus: 70

Govinda £ ❹ Delicious, cheap curries and sweets from the quietly efficient Hare Krishnas. ⓐ Obchodná 30 ❶ 02 5296 2366 ⓦ www.govinda.sk ❶ 11.00–20.00 Mon–Fri, 11.30–17.00 Sat ⓝ Tram: 5, 7, 9, 13

Dobrá Čajovňa ££ ❺ Grab a spot to recline and infuse the afternoon away. ⓐ Kollárovo nám 16 ⓦ www.dobracajka.sk ❶ 14.00–22.00 Mon–Fri, 16.00–22.00 Sat & Sun

Steam & Coffee ££ ❻ This chain provides well-priced healthy food and delicious coffee and teas. Classic. ⓐ Miletičova 23 ❶ 0918 631 785 ⓦ www.steamandcoffee.sk ❶ 08.00–22.00 Mon–Fri (Sat & Sun takeaway only) ⓝ Tram: 8, 9, 14

AFTER DARK

RESTAURANTS
Chez David ££ ❼ Jewish meals but not a kosher kitchen in this popular eatery with excellent selection of Slovak and Jewish wines. ⓐ Zámocká 13 ❶ 02 5441 3824 ⓦ www.chezdavid.sk ❶ 11.30–23.00 ⓝ Tram: 1, 5, 6, 7, 9

Film Restaurant ££ ❽ Popular Italian restaurant attached to the hotel of the same name and theme. Try the cocktail bar next door. ⓐ Vysoká 27 ❶ 02 5293 2794 ⓦ www.filmhotel.sk ❶ 10.00–23.00 Mon–Sat, 11.00–23.00 Sun ⓝ Tram: 1, 5, 6, 7, 9

Kikaku ££ ❾ Recommended sushi spot with only seafood and veg offerings. Discount available between 15.00–18.00 Mon–Fri.

ⓐ Gorkého 6 ⓣ 02 5443 4783 ⓦ www.kikaku.sk ⓛ 11.30–23.00
Mon–Fri, 17.00–23.00 Sat, 17.00–22.00 Sun Ⓝ Tram: 4, 12, 13, 14

U Melónka ££ ❿ A wide variety of Slovakian and international
food, with an emphasis on delicious fish and pizza, is offered at
this charming and authentic eatery. ⓐ Malý trh 2/A ⓣ 02 3352 6994
ⓦ www.umelonka.sk ⓛ 08.00–23.00 Mon–Fri, 10.00–23.00 Sat
& Sun Ⓝ Trolleybus: 206, 208

Modrá hviezda ££ ⓫ Beautiful 18th-century building with
nook and cranny dining and traditional regional cuisine
that inspires oohs and aahs. ⓐ Beblavého 14 ⓣ 02 5443 2747
ⓦ www.modrahviezda.sk ⓛ 11.30–23.00

Restaurant Matyšák ££ ⓬ Superb. Impeccable service.
More than 4,000 bottles of wine in the cellar plus traditional
Slovak musical accompaniment. ⓐ Pražská 15 ⓣ 02 2063 4053
ⓦ www.hotelmatysak.sk ⓛ 07.00–10.00, 11.30–22.00 Ⓝ Bus: 32,
34, 41, 83, 84; trolleybus: 204, 206, 209, 212

Santé ££ ⓭ Friendly if a little sterile neighbourhood bistro
and restaurant that delivers excellent thin crust pizzas and
bowls of delicious pasta plus breakfast and enchiladas.
ⓐ Dunajská 34 ⓦ www.santerestaurant.sk ⓛ 08.00–23.00
Ⓝ Trolleybus: 202, 205

Trafená Hus ££ ⓮ The sophisticated Czech pub chain (from
Prague brewery Staropramen) comes to Bratislava. Hearty dishes
washed down with a large selection of beer. ⓐ Šafarikovo nám 7

① 0911 311 777 ⓦ www.trafenahus.sk ⓛ 08.00–00.00 Mon–Thur, 08.00–01.00 Fri, 11.00–01.00 Sat, 11.00–00.00 Sun

Traja mušketieri ££ ⑮ Ritzy cellar with costumed waiting staff serving delicious period dishes (d'Artagnan's Sword) to a happy crowd of wealthy locals, expats and tourists. ⓐ Sládkovičova 7 ① 02 5443 0019 ⓦ www.trajamusketieri.sk ⓛ 11.00–23.00

Caribic's £££ ⑯ This venue is rightly renowned for its seafood. Look for the dolphin mural and lovely winter garden. ⓐ Žižkova 1/A ① 02 5441 8334 ⓦ www.caribics.sk ⓛ 11.00–00.00 ⓝ Tram: 4, 12, 17

U Mamičky £££ ⑰ Gorgeous garden with grill makes a delightful summer place, but superb seafood and homemade flat bread make this a perfect stop any day. ⓐ Palisady 40 ① 02 5443 4618 ⓦ www.umamicky.sk ⓛ 11.30–22.00 ⓝ Trolleybus: 203, 207, 208

UFO £££ ⑱ This iconic place has somewhat painted plate (great presentation, little substance) Mediterranean/Asian cuisine, but good cocktails and the view cannot be beaten. ⓐ Nový most ① 02 6252 0300 ⓦ www.u-f-o.sk ⓛ 10.00–23.00

BARS
Hysteria Pub Mexican food and a weekend disco. ⓐ Odbojárov 9, off Staromestká ① 0905 529 995 ⓦ www.pub.sk ⓛ 09.00–01.00 Mon–Thur, 11.00–05.00 Fri & Sat, 11.00–00.00 Sun ⓝ Bus: 39, 53, 61, 63, 74, 78; tram: 2, 4; trolleybus: 204, 205

◆ Nový most with its famous UFO-shaped restaurant

Maňana A local laid back favourite where you might never see tomorrow on a good night. ⓐ Kollárovo nám. 15 ⓣ 0915 548 099 ⓦ www.mananapub.sk ⓛ 17.00–05.00 ⓝ Bus: 34, 31, 39, 94; tram: 9, 5, 7, 13; trolleybus: 206, 207, 208, 212

Plzenská Superb Czech pub food and beers from this traditional cellar bar named after Plzen, the town in which Pilsner Urquell was invented. ⓐ Rajská 5 ⓣ 02 5292 0610 ⓛ 10.00–00.00 Sun & Mon, 10.00–01.00 Tues–Thur, 11.00–02.00 Fri & Sat ⓝ Tram: 4, 7, 11, 14, 17; trolleybus: 202, 205

Radost Chill Out Small bar with DJs and friendly folk. Arab cuisine and sheesha fuel the atmosphere. ⓐ Obchodná 48 ⓣ 0907 723 678 ⓦ www.mojaradost.sk ⓛ 17.00–05.00 ⓝ Tram: 5, 7, 9, 13

Slovak Pub A huge pub that manages to be a tourist trap *and* local hangout. History, food and beer in raucous surroundings. Reservations recommended. ⓐ Obchodná 62 ⓣ 02 5292 6367 ⓦ www.slovakpub.sk ⓛ 10.00–00.00 Mon–Thur, 10.00–02.00 Fri & Sat, 12.00–00.00 Sun ⓝ Tram: 5, 7, 9, 13

LIVE MUSIC

Hostinec Umelka The pub with a massive beer garden, kilos of grilled meat and some of the best live music in the city. ⓐ Dostojevského rad 2 ⓣ 02 5263 4754 ⓦ www.umelka.sk ⓛ 10.00–00.00 Mon–Thur, 10.00–01.00 Fri, 11.00–01.00 Sat, 11.00–00.00 Sun ⓝ Bus: 50, 95; tram: 4, 12, 11, 13, 14

Devín Castle & Greater Bratislava

Although a trip to Devín is a must, the other attractions available further out of the city will probably only be seen by those with some time on their hands. These off-the-beaten-path attractions underline all that the city is unknown for. Discover the hidden Bratislava outside the historical centre.

SIGHTS & ATTRACTIONS

Bobová Dráha (Bobsleigh track)

Fantastic fun with the frisson of speed and some danger, the bobsleigh track using carts on wheels. A ski lift services the slope in winter. ☎ 0918 683 202 ⓦ www.bkteam.sk/bobo ⏰ 10.00–18.00 summer; 10.00–18.00 Sat & Sun, winter ⓝ Trolleybus: 203 then walk up hill for about 20 minutes. Admission charge (minimum of five people)

Botanická zahráda (Botanical Gardens)

The Botanical Gardens and *skleníky* (greenhouse), part of the Univerzita Komenského, are cheap and delightful. The greenhouse holds various tropical and desert species, while the gardens are a fiesta of native and exotic plants. There's also a Japanese Garden. ⓐ Botanická 3 ☎ 02 6542 5440 ⏰ 09.00–18.00 Apr–Oct; *Skleníky:* 09.00–15.00 Mon–Fri, 09.00–18.00 Sat & Sun, Apr–Oct ⓝ Bus: 28, 29, 32, 133; tram: 1, 4, 5, 9, 12, 17; turn left over the footbridge

Bratislava Zoo & DinoPark

Set in 96 hectares (237 acres) of Carpathian farmland, the zoo, with more than 1,396 animals from 174 species is more than just a viewing platform. The Rehabilitation Station rescues injured and ailing animals from the wild and an education centre proves it's never too early to instil a sense of responsibility for animals and the environment we must all share. The DinoPark, an exhibition of scale replicas of various dinosaurs, is unique to Central Europe and fascinating for kids of all ages. ⓐ Mlynská dolina 1 ⓣ 02 6542 0985 or 6010 2111 ⓦ www.zoobratislava.sk ⓛ 09.00–18.00 May–Oct; 10.00–15.00 Nov–Apr ⓝ Bus: 30, 31, 32, 37, 39, 92, 131, 192 (bus stop Slávičie údolie for 31 and 39, Zoo for others). Admission charge

Hrad Devín (Devín Castle)

Devín Castle is the historical and cultural heart of the Slovak nation. It is a history lesson in itself, dating back to 5000 BC and

ⓞ Devín Castle is central to the Slovak story

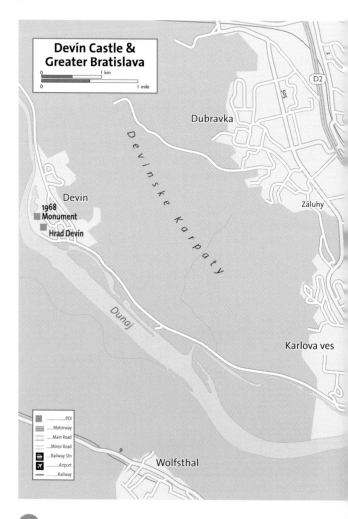

Devín Castle & Greater Bratislava

0   1 km
0   1 mile

D2

505

2

Dubravka

Záluhy

Devín

1968 Monument

Hrad Devín

Devinske Karpaty

Dunaj

Karlova ves

POI
Motorway
Main Road
Minor Road
Railway Stn
Airport
Railway

9

Wolfsthal

Podháj

Malokarpatské

Lanovka

Železná
studnička

Lamač

Rázsochy

TV Tower

Lanoland

Bobová
Dráha

Kamzik
439

Mestské lesy
v Bratislave

Briežky

Koliba

Červený most

Vtáčnik

Kútiky

Vinohrady

Bratislava Zoo
& DinoPark

Bratislava-
Hlavná

M.R Štefánika

Slavín
Monument

Staré mesto

BRATISLAVA

Botanická
zahráda

505

D2

Roman Bratislava &
Danubiana Meulensteen
Art Museum

Dunaj

N

continuing via the Celts, Romans and Hungarians to Napoleon, who – in typical fashion – blew it up in 1809.

The path to the castle is steep and there are many steps, but the history, museums and views are stupendous. Devín sits on a 212 m (695 ft) cliff above the confluence of the Danube and the Moravia rivers, making it the perfect spot for a fortress. After initial settlement in neolithic times, the Celts arrived, followed by the Romans – the Limes Romanus ran along the Danube as the border of the Roman Empire. The slanted building on the way up to the castle holds the remains of the oldest Christian building north of the Danube, the *cella memoriae*, which was unearthed in 1975. It is assumed to be a wooden-roofed Roman chapel, rebuilt many times – indicating extended use. The castle has four gates: Devín Gate, Bratislava and Danube Gates, and Moravia Gate (where the ticket office is now situated). Remains of Slav houses, with their fireplaces in the corner of the house rather than the more usual centre, flank the path, and there are benches to rest and enjoy the view. The facing hillside, Devínska Kobyla, is the edge of the Small Carpathian Mountains and is a protected area for its biodiversity.

In 863, two Byzantine priests – Cyril and Methodius – were sent by their Emperor, Michael III, to convert the barbarian hordes of Greater Moravia and by doing so broke the Slav nation from German dominance and language. It is thought that Cyril and Methodius established a school in the castle to teach the Slav alphabet they devised. Another reason for Devín's national importance is due to Ľudovít Štúr, who led a quest for Slovak national statehood and created the Slav language standard. There is a plaque commemorating him and the meeting that took place here on 24 April 1836. A nearby exhibition space shows archaeological, cultural and historical finds from the castle grounds over the (numerous) years.

Štúr's quest was not successful at that time, and at the end of the 19th century a column was erected in the castle to honour The Hungarian Soldier, anathema to the Slovaks in this hallowed place of Slav national identity. In 1921 the column was bombed. The only remaining evidence that it stood is a photo in the museum in the upper massif section of the castle.

Devín Castle has three sections: the lower Gothic section built and inhabited by the Gara family; the middle section, with the well and Roman foundations built by the Bartok family in the Renaissance style; and the upper massif section once surrounded by a moat built by the baroque-era Pálffy family. The museum in the massif depicts the changes undergone at Devín under these families, to whom the castle was leased by the ruling dukes of the day.

From the highest point of the massif, popular today for weddings, one can see the natural protection afforded the site with two rivers and the cliff leaving only one side to be fortified. A pictorial plaque shows Devín's place on this strategic junction relative to other castles in the vicinity. Looking down to the smaller Moravia River, the white stone '1968 Monument' is dedicated to those who attempted to swim the Danube to the west and free themselves from Communism (but were shot or drowned). The Iron Curtain Greenway and Moravia River Flood Plain Greenway provide lovely walking or biking paths. Bratislava is just 9 km (6 miles) away and visiting Devín makes a lovely day out on bikes.

The parking area has basic restaurants and beer gardens for the weary castle visitor and there's another outlet in the castle grounds too. ⓐ Muránska ulitsa ⓣ 02 6573 0105 ⓛ Castle: 10.00–17.00 Mon–Fri, 10.00–19.00 Sat & Sun, May–Sept; 10.00–17.00 Tues–Sun, Apr, Oct–Nov; Ruins: 10.00–17.00 Dec–Mar ⓝ Bus: 29. Admission charge

Lanoland

Conquer your fear of heights and add to your self-confidence with this superb ropes course. With harnesses and instructors, it's safe and available for kids too. ⓐ Next to the Bobsleigh (see page 92) ⓣ 02 4363 5120 ⓦ www.lanoland.sk ⓛ 15.00–18.30 Tues–Fri, 10.00–18.30 Sat & Sun (closed in bad weather). Admission charge

Lanovka

The ski lift trundles up and down the slope to Kamzík, running each hour on the hour. ⓣ 02 4425 9188 ⓦ www.lanovky.sk ⓛ 10.00–18.00 May–Sept; 10.00–17.00 Thur & Fri, 10.00–18.00 Sat & Sun, Oct–Apr. Admission charge (under 5s free).

Mestské lesy v Bratislave (Bratislava City Forest), Koliba & Kamzík

The Small Carpathian Mountains drift down almost into Bratislava itself, and provide a respite from Slovakia's capital's increasingly urban lifestyle with walking, biking, hiking and ski trails. This Mestské lesy v Bratislave (Bratislava City Forest) is pinpointed by Kamzík, the TV Tower at Koliba, which was built in 1975 and towers 200 m (656 ft) above ground level. It reaches the dizzy heights of 638 m (2,093 ft) above sea level, however, allowing visitors a superb view of Austria, Hungary and the Czech Republic.

The city forest is a draw to outdoorsy people all year round as it is home to some easy ski slopes with a chair lift and ski pulls as well. The bobsleigh track and high ropes that cross at the summit provide entertainment for all the family, and a trail has been created from Červený most (Red Bridge) to Kamzík along lovely paths and past bubbling brooks and lakes, which become ice hockey practice paradise in winter.

Getting to Kamzík takes some dedication – unless you go by car or taxi, in which case it's simple but you haven't enjoyed the great outdoors. A good round trip is to take bus 204 or 207 to the last stop, then traverse the E65 highway via the underpass to Patrónka bus stop, take bus 43 and hop off at any stop once you are in the forest. You will see the City Forest maps and

● *The village of Devín spied from the castle massif*

legends at various points along the trail here, which basically follows the road. Walk the trail or hop off the bus at Lanovka in the Železná studnička area, where the ski lift ascends to the summit of Kamzík. You can walk the trails, too, if you are feeling fit. There are numerous campfire sites, gazebos, BBQ grills, picnic tables and kids' playgrounds along the way.

Once at the summit, explore the various sights and activities, have dinner at one of the restaurants, or sip a cold beer or hot wine while taking in the view from one of the kiosk-type affairs. The easiest way back is to follow the road down the city side of the mountain to catch bus 203, which will take you into the city centre in about 20 minutes.

Náučný chodník

The nature trail (which is what 'Náučný chodník' means) from Červený most (Red Bridge) to Kamzík, or vice versa, with information dotted along the way on flora, fauna, history, ecology, etc. Various walking and biking trails are laid out all over the city forest and they do advise sticking to trails as unexploded ordnance from World War II remains in the area. Follow the rules: don't damage the environment, don't litter and don't inadvertently start a wildland fire. Maps and info can be obtained at tourist information offices in Bratislava (see page 136) ❶ 02 5478 9035 (only reachable 08.00–16.00 Mon–Fri) ⓦ www.ba-lesy.sk

Slavín Monument

The 52 m (171 ft) Slavín Monument is dedicated to the soldiers of the Red Army who died in the liberation of the Slovak lands in World War II. An evocative monument that arouses passion to this day, it was unveiled on 4 April 1960 and depicts a Soviet soldier with flag standing on a Nazi swastika around which lie 278 individual graves, although the remains of 6,850 soldiers were brought here. *Slava* means 'glory', and, despite the later yoke of Communism after liberation by Russia's Red Army, this is a sacred place. Bratislavans often walk up here to sit, drink, think and watch their city, but always with respect for these fallen soldiers.

To get here, either walk uphill from Palisady or take bus 203 to the end of the line (at Búdková by the Zlatý Bažant Grill). Then walk along Stará vinárska to the monument, passing by a superb view of the city and some rather ritzy modern villas, including the US ambassador's residence, nicknamed the Little White House.

CULTURE

Danubiana Meulensteen Art Museum

Some 15 km (9 miles) south of Bratislava is the modern art museum set in beautiful grounds on an island in the mighty Danube. Opened in 2000 and designed by architect Peter Zalman, this unique gallery is shaped like a Roman galley and has some 2,000 sq m (6,550 sq ft) of exhibition space, not including the pieces on show in the extensive grounds. The collection here is continually added to and includes works by Slovak and international artists all with some link to the Meulensteen Foundation. Join the likes of King Juan Carlos of Spain and wander around this massive and welcome newcomer to the art scene. There is a shop and café on the premises. ⓐ Vodné dielo, Čunovo ① 02 6252 8501 ⓦ www.danubiana.sk ⓛ 10.00–20.00

Tues–Sun, May–Sept; 10.00–18.00 Tues–Sun, Oct–Apr ⊘ Bus: 91, 191 to Čunovo; the 3 km (2 mile) walk to the museum is signposted. Admission charge

Roman Bratislava

Oh, how the mighty are fallen. In the Bratislavan suburb of Rusovce is Antická Gerulata, a museum on the site of one of the furthest garrisons of the Roman military, in the province of Panonia, the border of which ran along the single line that was the Danube, the Limes Romanus and the edge of the empire itself. Gerulata

THE MOTHER-IN-LAW OF EUROPE: MARIA THERESA (1717–1780)

The above nickname came about after she strategically married off all her 16 children allowing only herself and favourite daughter Maria Kristina to marry for love. Late portraits of Maria Theresa show her continually clad in black following her husband's death. All her 11 daughters bore the first name Maria and her youngest daughter was Maria Antonia, better known under her French name Marie Antoinette.

Maria Theresa was one of the so-called 'enlightened despots' and bestowed on Bratislava the great honour of deciding it would be the summer seat of the royal family. She also decreed the moat and walls surrounding Bratislava to be filled in and torn down to make way for a growing populace, and thus a baroque building boom flourished.

dates back to the first century and excavations have revealed it as an important military position at an economically strong settlement. Gerulata is marked on the medieval copy of the fourth-century map *Tabula Peutingeriana*. Explore the excavations, burial grounds and skeletal remains. A Roman games festival is held in the summer. ⓐ Gerulatská 69 ⓣ 02 6285 9332 ⓛ 10.00–17.00 June–Oct ⓝ Bus: 91, 191; alternatively, follow the cycle route south along the Danube. Admission charge

RETAIL THERAPY

Avion Shopping Park Mall life has impacted here – check out IKEA and ice skating. ⓐ Ivanská cesta 16 ⓣ 02 4822 6800 ⓦ www.avion.sk ⓛ 10.00–21.00 ⓝ Bus: 61, 63, 67 plus free shuttle buses from Petržalka

AFTER DARK

RESTAURANTS
Modrý Dom ££ ❶ About half an hour from the city centre, this is a lovely village restaurant featuring superb Slovak cuisine (including the autumnal goose feast) and the wines the surrounding area is rightly famous for. For an alternative dessert, grab a cone from one of the best ice cream parlours around. ⓐ Roľnícka 56, Vajnory ⓣ 02 4371 1041 ⓦ www.modrydom.sk ⓛ 11.00–22.00 ⓝ Bus: 52, 53, 54, 56, 65

Reštaurácia Koliba-Expo ££ ❷ Traditional Slovak hospitality and cuisine in a sublime rural setting. Large terrace and open grill

add to the culinary delights. ⓐ Kamzíkov vrch ⓣ 02 5477 1764
ⓦ www.koliba-expo.sk ⓛ 11.00–00.00 ⓝ Trolleybus: 203 to the
last stop, then a 20-minute walk

Veža ££ ❸ Enjoy a 360° vista while slowly revolving high atop
Kamzík and dining on well-presented dishes. Some tables are
static but your fellow diners won't be. ⓐ Cesta na Kamzík 14
ⓣ 02 4446 2774 ⓦ www.veza.sk ⓛ 11.00–00.00

BARS & CLUBS

Harley Davidson Saloon Being on the wrong side of the
tracks and by a cemetery hasn't deadened this bikers' club –
probably because it's great – grill, terrace and twice nightly strip
shows, male and female. ⓐ Rebarborová 1/A ⓣ 0917 700 000
ⓦ www.harley-davidson.sk ⓛ 11.00–02.00 Sun–Thur, 11.00–06.00
Fri & Sat ⓝ Bus: 75; trolleybus: 201, 202, 208

Route 69 Taking a lesson from the film, the girls dance on the bar,
get the punters well watered and bestow a great evening on a
grateful crowd. ⓐ Rožňavská 1 ⓣ 0918 187 689 ⓦ www.route69.sk
ⓛ 08.00–23.00 Mon–Thur, 08.00–05.00 Fri, 10.00–05.00 Sat
ⓝ Bus: 53, 63

▶ *A swathe of autumn colours cover the foothills of the Small Carpathians*

Malokarpatské (Small Carpathian Mountains)

Heading out of Bratislava on Račianska street, known as Victorious February 1948 street during the Communist regime, leads you to the Small Carpathians. This mountain range begins at Devín and, under various names including Slovakia's High Tatras, arches into Ukraine and Romania. The southern slopes are lined with vines.

GETTING THERE

Bratislava's tourist information office (see page 136) organises Wine Route tours to the towns and sights mentioned, making it easy to do in a half day. That said, intrepid folk can drive or take a bus from Bratislava's Autobusova stanica on Mlynské Nivy. The journey to Častá (for Červený kameň) on the bus takes 1 hour 20 minutes, but the bus does stop at all the following places in the Small Carpathians. Bus travellers will need at least two days to see all of the following.

SIGHTS & ATTRACTIONS

SVÄTÝ JUR

The picturesque town of St George is just 14 km (9 miles) from Bratislava but retains its village feel. The first written record of St George dates to 1209, although there has been a settlement here since the fourth millennium BC. The town gained full royal privileges in 1615 and reached its golden period when its wines were exported across the region. Original vintners' houses remain around the square, which are characterised by the large central door allowing carriages of grapes to enter the courtyard and production to begin. The town has a number of historical sites: the Gothic 13th-century Church of St George, which holds a white sandstone altar and painting of St George slaying the dragon, plus tombs and sarcophagi. Also, check out the 17th-century wooden bell tower. The ruins of 13th-century Biely Kameň (White Rock Castle) are a 30-minute hike through the forest and are a popular summer destination. There is also a free outdoor pool open in the summer from 08.00–18.00.

○ *The dramatic landscape of the Small Carpathian Mountains*

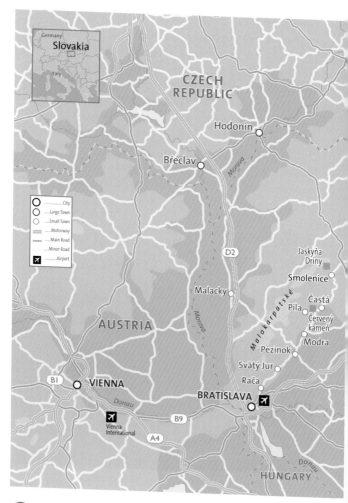

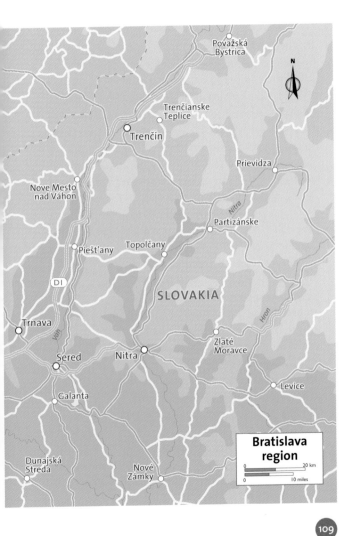

IN VINO VERITAS

The Celts produced wine in this region centuries ago, then better vines arrived with the migration of nations towards the end of the Roman Empire. However, it wasn't until Bratislava became the capital of the Hungarian Empire that the region's wines gained in reputation – after being sipped by the lips of royalty. During Communism, quality declined as vineyards were nationalised and only two variations, red and white, were pressed. Nowadays, these wines are once again winning awards. Wines from generations of wine-making families have won the most accolades. Those listed below (and others) provide tours of cellars and samples of wine accompanied by bread, cheese and *oškvarkova masť* (pork dripping).

Hacaj ⓐ Cajlanská 66, Pezinok ⓣ 033 640 2696
ⓦ www.hacaj.sk

Hubert ⓐ Vinárska 137, Sereď ⓣ 031 788 1039
ⓦ www.hubertsekt.sk

Matyšák ⓐ Holubyho 85, Pezinok ⓣ 033 640 9023
ⓦ www.vinomatysak.sk

Mrva & Stanko ⓐ Orešianska 7/A, Trnava ⓣ 033 591 4741
ⓦ www.mrvastanko.sk

Pavelka ⓐ Cajlanská 126, Pezinok ⓣ 033 641 1065
ⓦ www.pavelkavino.sk

September is the month to travel to this hilly domain as it is the month of *vinobranie*, the *burčiak* (young wine) festival. Carnivores must try *husacina* (the accompanying roast goose feast) and *lokše* (potato pancakes). St Martin's Day, 11 November, sees the new wine being blessed and, of course, sampled, and 17–18 November hosts Open Cellar Days where for a small charge you get a map, glass and, best of all, to sample wines from dozens of cellars between Rača and Trnava.

As well as ordinary wine, look out for bottles of ice wine – a type of dessert wine made from grapes frozen while still on the vine.

Information centre ⓐ Prostredná 64 ⓣ 02 4497 0449
ⓦ www.svatyjur.sk ⓛ 14.00–19.00 Mon–Sat

PEZINOK

Pezinok is 18 km (11 miles) from Bratislava, is the regional centre and was first mentioned, as Terra Bozen, in written documents in 1208. Originally a mining town, it became a vintner's paradise in the 16th century. In 1647 the town was awarded royal privileges, and the next two centuries saw Pezinok's fame boom due to its superlative wines, industry and railway resulting in a beautiful town with much to see. Pezinok Castle has no museum but does have an excellent restaurant (see page 118) and an exhibit featuring the best 100 Slovak wines – with the possibility to sample and buy.

Information centre ⓐ Holubyho 42 ⓣ 033 640 69 89
ⓦ www.pezinok.sk

MODRA

Modra is 25 km (15 miles) from Bratislava and, as with most towns in the region, signs of settlement reach back to around 3000 BC but remains of a castle in nearby Harmonia and a burial ground to the northeast of the town point to permanent settlements since the ninth century. Modra was conferred the status of Free Royal Town in 1607. Soon afterwards the town built its fortifications with three gateways; some sections plus the Horná brána (Upper Gate) remain. The entire area is crossed by trails for hiking, biking and horse riding, and ski lifts operate all winter.

Information centre ⓐ Štúrova 59 ⓣ 033 647 2312 ⓦ www.modra.sk

Evanjelický kostol apoštolov Petra a Pavla (Church of Peter & Paul)

This Lutheran church is located outside the old city walls as law stated that only Catholic churches were allowed inside the city walls. ⓐ Dolná, Modra

Kostol svätého Štefana Kráľa (Church of St Stephan the King)

This was initially only the clock tower; the church was added later. ⓐ Corner of Štúrova & Dukelská, Modra

ČERVENÝ KAMEŇ (Red Rock Castle)

The magnificent Red Rock Castle is the best preserved castle in Slovakia thanks largely to the Pálffy family who lived here from 1583 until 1945, when they abandoned their seat. The castle, so called for the red rock it is built on, rather than of, gradually deteriorated until the 1950s when it was declared a Slovak National Monument and a massive 20-year restoration project began.

Continued warring led to the various Pálffys travelling far overseas, and as was the trend for the period, they brought home spoils of war, art, furniture and medicines. The exhibitions inside the castle, which are only accessible with a tour, show the eclectic and enlightened side of the family.

There is so much to see in this amazing castle. The weird folly room with pebble mosaic floor and waterfalls was used to cool down on hot days. The Turkish curved dagger was used for beheadings with an inner section to slice off ears. Then there's the fireplace and war emblems in the Knights' Room. The cellars, used by the Pálffys for wine, are the largest in Europe.

One of the castle's bastions is open for all to marvel at its sheer size. There are four interior floors with various windows for various weapons to be used in defence, the central support and huge ventilation shafts. Think of all the gunpowder! The

⏺ *The courtyard of Červený kameň*

extensive grounds can be explored any time and keep an eye out for the albino peacock. On the last Saturday of each month, the castle courtyard holds an outdoor antique market (🕒 07.00–12.00). The summer brings horses and ponies to ride plus various historical fencing, jousting and cultural re-enactments. Additionally, night tours show an illuminating side of the castle.

The castle has no heating, so be prepared if you are visiting in winter. Tours in English are by appointment only, and there is a charge. That said, you can join a Slovak-language tour and use a printed sheet for limited information. ⓐ Častá, 35 km (22 miles) from Bratislava 🕾 033 690 5803 🌐 www.snm.sk 🕒 09.00–18.00 May–Aug; 09.00–17.00 Sat & Sun, Mar, Apr, Sept & Oct. Admission charge

COAT OF ARMS

The courtyard fountain at Červený kameň shows the Pálffy coat of arms – a stag rising from a wheel – which is also the emblem for Bratislava. The story, for the Pálffys anyway, is that one dark and stormy night, when the family were on their way home, a stag leapt out of the forest breaking their carriage wheel and forcing them to remain there that night. As daylight illuminated their predicament, it became apparent that the stag had actually saved their lives as the carriage (purportedly the one on show inside the castle) was on the edge on an abyss. However, despite this stag saving their skins, it appears the Pálffys didn't reciprocate the favour, judging from all the hides and heads hammered to their walls.

Astur Falconry ⓐ Hrad Červený Kameň ☏ 033 690 5827
ⓦ www.falconry.sk 🕓 10.00–17.00 15 Mar–31 Oct only;
raptor shows at 11.45, 14.15 & 16.15. Admission charge

CULTURE

PEZINOK
Gallery of Naïve Art

Schaubmar Mill was built in 1767 by the Pálffy family. It was
then acquired in the 19th century by the Schaubmar family,
who kept it working until the early 20th century. The Slovak
National Gallery has reconstructed the exterior and renovated
the interior, which is a superb and functional technical
museum. Sadly, though, the waterwheel is broken. This fine
gallery of Slovak and international naïve art was established
in 1997. ⓐ Cajlanská 255 ☏ 033 640 4035 ⓦ www.sng.sk
🕓 10.00–17.00 Tues–Sun. Admission charge

Malokarpatské muzeum

This museum is located in a vintner's house and tells the history
of the town and winemaking – generously doling out samples of the
latter. ⓐ M R Štefánika 4 ☏ 033 641 3347 ⓦ www.muzeumpezinok.sk
🕓 09.00–12.00, 13.00–17.00 Tues–Fri, 09.00–15.00 Sat,
13.00–17.00 Sun

Stará radnica (Old Town Hall)

The Old Town Hall holds the city museum, a gallery and café. The
Mariansky stíp column was hidden through Communist times
and re-erected after the Velvet Revolution. ⓐ M R Štefánika 1

033 641 2306 www.pezinok.sk 10.00–12.00, 13.30–18.00 Tues–Fri, 10.00–16.00 Sat

MODRA

In the 16th century the Habáni, or Anabaptists, aroused the ire of the Habsburg lawmakers and fled Switzerland. These commune-minded, introverted craftsmen arrived in the area and introduced Modra to their method of ceramic-making. While many potters and painters work at the cooperative in Modra, you can also drop in on one of seven or so independent craftsmen for an unscheduled visit to their workshop. Watch the fluid lines of the objects appear on the potter's wheel. See the changes wrought after kilning and observe the art of detailed freehand painting. Tinkers, master wire craftsmen, can fix cracked and broken pots, dishes and jugs but as people tend to just buy another one nowadays, they have

A surreal perspective, a Modra ceramics workshop

extended their craft into producing intricate art and objects.

Miroslav Malinovský

Superb shop and workshop featuring his ceramics plus the works
of other artists and kids he teaches. ⓐ Štúrova 60 ❶ 0903 796 474
ⓦ www.tik.sk ⓛ 09.00–18.00 Mon–Fri, 09.00–12.00 Sat

Múzeum Ľudovíta Štúra

National leader, linguist and MP who retired, died and is buried
here. ⓐ Štúrova 83 ❶ 033 647 2765 ⓦ www.snm.sk ⓛ 08.00–16.00
Tues–Fri, 09.00–15.00 Tues–Sat, Apr–Oct

Slovenská ľudová majolika

The ceramics cooperative. Call in advance for a tour. ⓐ Dolná 138
❶ 033 647 2941 ⓦ www.majolika.sk ⓛ 08.00–11.00, 13.00–15.00
Mon–Fri. Admission charge

TAKING A BREAK & AFTER DARK

SVÄTÝ JUR

Korzo £ Right in the centre of town, this restaurant and bar
offers a scrumptious lunch menu, as well as pizzas and salads.
ⓐ Prostredná 29 ❶ 0903 760 535 ⓦ www.korzo.sk ⓛ 11.00–23.00
Mon–Thur, 11.00–01.00 Fri, 11.00–03.00 Sat, 11.00–22.00 Sun

PEZINOK

Milan Bejdák Vinogallery ££ Superb cellar for sampling, drinking
and eating (but no smoking). ⓐ Turecký dom, Radničné nám 1
❶ 0905 431 329 ⓦ www.vinogallery.sk ⓛ 16.00–23.00 Thur–Sat

Pezinok Castle ££ Why not try Zámocka in the impressive surroundings of the castle grounds? ⓐ Mladoboleslavská 5 ⓣ 033 641 2359 ⓦ www.zamockarestauracia.sk ⓛ 11.00–23.00

Radnica ££ Live jazz with your wine. ⓐ Štefánikova 1 ⓣ 033 641 4009 ⓦ www.radnica.com ⓛ 10.00–23.00 Mon–Thur, 10.00–02.00 Fri, 11.00–00.00 Sat, 12.00–23.00 Sun

Vinum Galéria Bozen ££ Reservations are a must at the Matyšak family's hostelry. ⓐ Holubyho 85 ⓣ 033 640 9023 ⓦ www.vinomatysak.sk ⓛ 17.00–23.00

MODRA
U Richtára ££ Popular and delightful restaurant in a classic vintner's home stocked with the renowned family wines. ⓐ Štúrova 93 ⓣ 033 6405 708 ⓦ www.urichtara.com ⓛ 11.00–22.00 Mon–Thur, 11.00–23.00 Fri & Sat

Vináreň u Ludvika ££ Wine cellar, restaurant and shop in one beautifully renovated 17th-century wine cellar with terrace, kids' play area and a wood-fire-heated private dining room. ⓐ Dukelská 2 ⓣ 0915 408 350 ⓦ www.vinoludvik.sk ⓛ 11.00–22.00 Mon–Sat, 11.00–21.00 Sun

ČERVENÝ KAMEŇ
The castle £ The café inside the castle courtyard is open when the castle is; there is also the Pod Bastou restaurant near the car park which is open 11.00–23.00.

ACCOMMODATION

SVÄTÝ JUR

Horský Hotel Eva £ Situated on the valley floor is this beautiful hotel with rooms, cottage, pub, horse riding, pool and skiing in winter. ⓐ Jozefkovo Údolie ⓣ 02 4497 0507 ⓦ www.horskyhotel-eva.sk

PEZINOK

Horský Hotel Istota ££ For a rural stay with a divine wine cellar, try here. It also offers horse riding and skiing. ⓐ Kučišdorfská dolina 2559 ⓣ 033 640 2937 ⓦ www.hotelistota.sk

Hotel Vinársky dom ££ This new hotel in the centre of town has various standards of rooms. ⓐ Holubyho 27 ⓣ 033 640 0933 ⓦ www.vinarskydom.sk

MODRA

Hotel Zochova chata £ A traditional Slovakian winter and summer resort, this is the hotel for outdoorsy people. An excellent restaurant but little English spoken. ⓐ Piesok ⓦ www.zochova-chata.com

Club MKM ££ Recommended *pension* with more services than you'd expect in Modra and a lovely restaurant. ⓐ Štúrova 25 ⓣ 033 647 2009 ⓦ www.slovenskehory.sk

ČERVENÝ KAMEŇ

Penzión Redrock 55 £ In the nearby village of Píla. ⓣ 0903 212 671

Further afield

Historically – and culturally – important towns abound in this area. In addition to the following destinations, don't forget that skiing takes place all over Slovakia with good slopes, snow and prices. See www.skislovakia.sk for information.

GETTING THERE

TRNAVA

Trnava lies some 40 km (25 miles) from Častá and is located at the end of the Small Carpathian Wine Route. It is a large town and the seat of the Catholic Archbishop. It is just 50 km (31 miles) from Bratislava and easily accessible by bus from the main bus station on Mlynské Nivy.

AROUND TRNAVA

Piešťany (85 km/53 miles from Bratislava and 35 km/22 miles from Trnava) has a small airport with connections to Bratislava, along with the more usual bus and train connections.

NITRA

Located 80 km (50 miles) from Bratislava it is well connected by bus from the capital's main bus station on Mlynské Nivy. The bus station in Nitra is about a 15-minute walk from the town centre.

TRENČÍN

Trenčín, some 100 km (62 miles) from Bratislava, is easily accessible from the city by car, bus and train.

SIGHTS & ATTRACTIONS

TRNAVA

Information centre This is on the ground floor of the Renaissance Mestká veža (City Tower) on Trojičné nám where the baroque Holy Trinity statue is located. ☎ 033 3236 440 ⓦ www.trnava.sk

St Nicolas (ⓐ Nám sv Mikulaša) and **St John the Baptist** (ⓐ Univerzitné nám) are just two of many notable churches.

Západoslovenské múzeum (Western Slovakia Museum)

Located in a 13th-century convent, this museum has cultural and historical exhibits from the region. ⓐ Muzejné nám 3 ☎ 033 551 2913 🕑 08.00–17.00 Tues–Fri, 11.00–17.00 Sat & Sun

🔺 *Trenčín Castle perched above the town*

AROUND TRNAVA
Cave formations

The karst landscape that exists under much of Slovakia, and particularly around the High Tatras, has created some spectacular cave formations. The closest cave to Bratislava is Jaskyňa Driny (Driny Cave), which has 410 m (1,345 ft) open to explore, from narrow fissures to medium-size caverns and fabulous sinter deposits. A bus followed by a short walk from Smolenice will take you to the caves. ☏ 033 558 6200 ⏰ Mon–Sat, Apr–Oct. Admission charge

Springs & spas

As a result of volcanic activity in the Small Carpathians, there are hidden springs and curative waters bubbling around under the country. One such spa area is Piešťany. This spa resort (on Spa Island, no less) was founded in 1889 and lies in the valley of the Váh River. The water and mud treatments are renowned for their curative effects on arthritis particularly. If you book with a spa hotel, it will arrange transport from the capital. For information and reservations see ⓦ www.spapiestany.com or contact the **central booking office** ⓐ Winterova 29, Piešťany ☏ 033 775 7733 ⏰ 07.00–18.00 Mon–Fri

NITRA

The regional centre of Nitra is the oldest city in the country. It is home to the first Christian place of worship in Slovakia (built in 828) and is also where Cyril and Methodius located their school dedicated to the Slav/Slovak alphabet and language after they arrived in the area in 863.

Archaeological remains indicate this area was settled up to 30,000 years ago due to the fertile soil and Nitra is today an economic, cultural and agricultural centre. The tourist information centre will give information, maps and guided tours of the historical centre, which might be the best idea for a short visit here as there is much to see and do. Skiing, hiking and horse riding are popular outdoor pursuits and the good info people will help with these as well.

Nitra, like Rome, was built on seven hills and these make for lovely hikes. If you can only visit one, head for Zobor and follow the hour-long educational trail to the summit. Take bus 9 to the final stop for the start of the trail.

The central historical area is where you will find the Royal Way and the **Church of Sts Cyril & Methodius** (ⓐ Piaristická).

Tourist information ⓐ Štefánikova 1 ☎ 037 16 186 ⓦ www.nitra.sk & www.nisys.sk ⏰ 08.00–18.00 Mon–Fri, 08.00–12.00 Sat, Sept–June; 08.00–18.00 Mon–Fri, 09.00–18.00 Sat, 14.00–18.00 Sun, July & Aug

Regional Information Centre ⓐ Nábrežie mládeže 1 ☎ 037 7722 400 ⓦ www.rpic.sk ⏰ 08.00–18.00 Mon–Fri, 08.00–12.00 Sat, Sept–June; 08.00–18.00 Mon–Fri, 09.00–18.00 Sat, 14.00–18.00 Sun, July & Aug

Nitriansky hrad (Nitra Castle)

This building dominates the landscape. Its cathedral is in the Upper Town, where the Bishop's Palace and the Great and Small Seminaries are located. Here you will also find a lovely city park and the **Statue of Corgoň** (ⓐ Pribinovo nám), who was supposed to have saved the castle from the Turks and has the locally brewed beer named after him. ☎ 037 7721 724 ⏰ 09.00–12.00, 13.00–18.00 Mon–Sat, 10.00–12.00, 14.00–17.00 Sun, Apr–Oct; 09.00–12.00, 13.00–16.00 Mon–Sat, 10.00–12.00, 14.00–16.00 Sun, Nov–Mar

Synagóga v Nitre (Nitra Synagogue)

The women's gallery of this former synagogue houses a poignant permanent exhibition of the Holocaust, put together by the Museum of Jewish Culture based in Bratislava. ⓐ Pri synagóge 3 ☎ 037 652 5320 ⓦ www.synagoga.sk ⏰ 13.00–18.00 Tues, Sat & Sun, 09.00–12.00, 13.00–18.00 Wed & Thur. Admission charge

Vasil Tower

At the cathedral, ask for the key to this tower to check out the spectacular view of the city and environs.

TRENČÍN

Trenčín is spectacularly pinpointed by its castle, one-time seat of the Mighty Lord of the Váh and the Tatras, Matúš Csák III. Don't miss the Roman inscription on the castle walls near the Hotel Tatra dating to the first century AD, nor the Renaissance parish stairway built in 1568. Trenčín is famous for its fashion designers and for the country's largest music festival at the airport in July. **Further information** ⓦ www.slktn.sk

Bažant Pohoda Festival

This attracts big names and thousands of spectators. The airport is almost limitless in capacity. Check for exact dates and line-up. ⓦ www.pohodafestival.sk

Katov dom (Executioner's House)

This incongruously picturesque property dates to 1580 and is one of the few medieval burgher houses remaining in Trenčín. ⓐ Matúšova 14 ⓒ 09.00–17.00 Tues–Sun, Apr–Nov. Admission charge

Trenčianske Teplice

Close by, this can be reached by train and bus from either Bratislava or Trenčín. It has an annual film festival held in June (ⓦ www.artfilm.sk) featuring films of all genres from all over the world. Whilst you're here visit the thermal pool and beautiful Moorish *hammam*.

🔺 *Church of St Peter Xaverský, Trenčín*

🔺 *Listening to a performance at the annual Trenčianske Teplice art film festival*

Trenčiansky hrad (Trenčín Castle)

This building remains the centre of things for culture (historical tournaments and festivities in the summer) and history (paintings, weapons and objects in museums in the castle and around town). ❶ 032 743 5657 ⓦ www.muzeumtn.sk ⏰ 09.00–17.00 Mar–Sept; 09.00–16.30 Oct; 09.00–15.30 Nov–Feb ❶ Tower closed in winter

Walking & biking

The River Váh and Lesopark Brezina provide ideal walking and bike trails. The excellent tourist information office provides info, souvenirs and tickets. ❸ Sládkovičova ❶ 032 16186 ⓦ www.trencin.sk ⏰ 08.00–18.00 Mon–Fri, 08.00–16.00 Sat, 1 May–30 Sept; 10.00–17.00 Mon–Fri, 10.00–12.00 Sat, 1 Oct–30 Apr

AFTER DARK

NITRA

Devil's Pub £ Get up to no good with the locals for a night's

drinking, partying or special event. @ Kmeťkova 2 ☏ 037 772 1392
🌐 www.devilspub.sk 🕐 20.00–01.00 Tues & Wed, 20.00–04.00
Fri & Sat

The Irish Times Pub £ Food, live music, good times and Guinness
all served in an authentic pub atmosphere. @ Kupecká 12
☏ 037 657 5106 🌐 www.irishtimespub.sk 🕐 08.00–01.00
Mon–Thur, 08.00–03.00 Fri & Sat, 11.00–00.00 Sun

TRENČÍN
Jameson Pub £ Good food, beer and weekend disco. @ Mierové
nám 13 ☏ 032 744 2061 🕐 09.00–00.00 Mon–Thur, 09.00–04.00
Fri, 16.00–04.00 Sat, 16.00–00.00 Sun

Korzár £ Excellent food is served in this pub restaurant that
delivers on all counts. @ J Braneckého 6 ☏ 032 649 1755
🕐 10.00–23.00 Mon–Thur, 10.00–01.00 Fri, 10.00–00.00 Sat,
11.00–23.00 Sun

ACCOMMODATION

TRNAVA
Hotel Barbakan ££ Standard rooms and services are made more
attractive by a good restaurant and lovely cellar pub with copper brew
tanks. @ Štefánikova 11 ☏ 033 5511 847 🌐 www.barbakan-trnava.sk

Hotel Dream ££ Well located in the historical centre, with
comfortable rooms, an excellent cellar restaurant and terrace.
@ Kapitulská 12 ☏ 033 592 4111 🌐 www.hoteldream.sk

NITRA

Hotel Átrium ££ Refurbished hotel in the city centre and with a winter garden restaurant. Internet and mod cons as standard. ⓐ Štefánikova 8 ⓣ 037 652 3790 ⓦ www.hotelatriumnitra.sk

Hotel Zlatý Kľúčik ££ Award-winning restaurant, lovely rooms and fitness centre/sauna on Zobor hill. ⓐ Svätourbanská 27 ⓣ 037 655 0289 ⓦ www.zlatyklucik.sk

ⓘ Trade fairs at the International Exhibition Centre double the price of accommodation, so to save money, make sure your visit doesn't coincide with one of them (ⓦ www.agrokomplex.sk).

TRENČÍN

Autocamping Na Ostrove £ Camp on an island surrounded by the Váh. ⓐ Na ostrove ⓣ 032 743 4013 ⓦ www.web.viaput.sk ⓛ 1 May–15 Sept

Hotel Brezina ££ Rural retreat for families and businessmen with buffet and outdoor BBQ pits. ⓐ M R Štefánika 19 ⓣ 032 652 8171 ⓦ www.hotel-brezina.sk

Hotel Tatra £££ Award-winning hotel and restaurant built by Baron Armin Popper in 1901 and superbly situated beneath the castle. ⓐ M R Stefánika 2 ⓣ 032 650 6111 ⓦ www.hotel-tatra.sk ⓛ Restaurant: 11.30–14.30, 18.00–22.00

ⓞ *Dragon signs denote pharmacies in the Old Town*

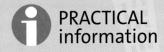

Directory

GETTING THERE

By air

Bratislava is served for national and international flights by
M R Štefánik airport. Ryanair and the Slovak low-cost carrier
SkyEurope fly here direct from many British and European cities.
Flying time from Britain is around two hours.

Ryanair ⓦ www.ryanair.com

SkyEurope ⓦ www.skyeurope.com

   International Airport Swechat (ⓦ www.viennaairport.com)
in Vienna is only 30 minutes from Bratislava, and the two cities
have excellent transport connections.

   Many people are aware that air travel emits CO_2, which
contributes to climate change. You may be interested in the
possibility of lessening the environmental impact of your flight
through the charity **Climate Care** (ⓦ www.climatecare.org),
which offsets your CO_2 by funding environmental projects
around the world.

By rail

With its prime location in the centre of Europe, Bratislava is well
linked with the rest of the continent by rail and this is how many
passengers currently arrive in the country. Slovakia's trains are
operated by **The Railways of the Slovak Republic** (ⓦ www.zsr.sk)
and all international trains arrive at Bratislava Hlavná stanica
(central train station). The search function for trains is in Slovak
and English at ⓦ www.slovakrail.sk. Alternatively, in the UK
visit **Rail Europe** (ⓐ 178 Piccadilly, London W1 ⓣ 08708 371 371

www.raileurope.co.uk). Journey time from the UK is about 24 hours.

By road

By road from Calais, head towards Dunkirk and cross the frontier into Belgium. From Belgium, you will journey all the way to Bratislava through the Netherlands, Germany and Austria on the E40. However, the road will have different numbers and letters in the various countries and, while it remains the E40, it may not always be called that.

ENTRY FORMALITIES

Visitors from the UK, Ireland, other EU countries, the USA, Canada, Australia and New Zealand need only a valid passport to enter the Slovak Republic and can stay for up to 90 days, although the entry visa as such is valid for 180 days. Visitors from South Africa must obtain a visa from an embassy or consulate before arriving in the country, and visas vary in cost.

MONEY

On 1 January 2009, Slovkia joined the euro (€) zone. There are banknotes in €5, €10, €20, €50, €100, €200 and €500 denominations, with coins for 1, 2, 5, 10, 20 and 50 cents and €1 and €2. Banks are open 09.00–18.00 Monday to Friday and 09.00–12.00 Saturday, but *bankomats* (ATMs) are prevalent. Money exchange offices also exist, but ATMs provide a much better rate of exchange. Do not try to break large notes in small shops or with taxi drivers.

HEALTH, SAFETY & CRIME

The water is safe to drink and there are no health issues for Bratislava. That said, as Slovakia is a landlocked country, you may want to be wary of shellfish. Hospitals are not quite up to British standards for cleanliness or facilities, but for emergencies (the treatment of which is free up to a limit) they are sufficient.

Crime is low on the radar for the average tourist, but be aware of potential pickpockets and cunning muggers in crowded areas. Items left unattended or on display will disappear. The police are armed and visible in green or blue uniforms but are not usually English-speaking.

OPENING HOURS

Shops 09.00–18.00 Monday to Friday
Malls and large shops 09.00–22.00
Post offices 08.00–17.00 Monday to Friday
Banks 09.00–18.00 Monday to Friday, 09.00–12.00 Saturday
Offices 09.00–17.00 Monday to Friday
Museums 09.00–18.00 Tuesday to Sunday
Restaurants The super economical Slovak lunch deal is served from 11.00–15.00, while kitchens usually close at 22.00.

TOILETS

Public toilets do exist, but you usually have to pay a few coins for the privilege of them having been cleaned and having toilet paper. Alternatively, pop into a café or restaurant, preferably buying something in return, or use the lobby facilities of one of the larger hotels.

CHILDREN

You might think kids and museums don't go together too well, but many of the exhibits in Bratislava are from its medieval past so weapons and torture instruments may well increase their level of interest. You can tire them out in the great outdoors with summer walks and winter tobogganing (any toy/sport shop sells cheap sledges) or at one of the numerous playgrounds around town.

Bibiana The International House of Art for Children where your kids can participate in one of the numerous events, workshops and dramas. The nearby graffiti is actually work done by the kids. Open invitation on Sat & Sun; call in advance for weekday activities. ⓐ Panská 41 ⓣ 02 5443 1308 ⓦ www.bibiana.sk ⓛ 10.00–18.00 Sat & Sun

Dráčik Local children's toy shop with huge selection and toys galore out of their boxes to be test-run. ⓐ Obchodná 2 ⓣ 02 5443 5456 ⓦ www.dracik.sk ⓛ 09.30–19.20 Mon–Fri, 09.00–14.00 Sat

Slovak National Gallery Call for details on its Kids' Creative Workshops. See page 85. ⓐ Rázusovo nábr 2 ⓣ 02 5443 2081 ⓦ www.sng.sk ⓛ 10.00–17.30 Tues–Sun

Bratislava Zoo & DinoPark Fascinating for kids of all ages. See page 92. ⓐ Mlynská dolina ⓣ 02 6542 0985 ⓦ www.zoobratislava.sk

COMMUNICATIONS

Internet

Most hotels now provide at least one free internet-enabled computer in the hotel lobby. If you have your own laptop or handheld device with you, there are numerous Wi-Fi spots in the city such as in Primaciálne nám, in front of the Primate's Palace. Internet cafes abound; here are just a couple:

Net Café Pay in advance and sign into your account.
ⓐ Obchodná 22 ☎ 02 5296 2847 🕒 09.00–00.00

Kristi@n Internet café, Wi-Fi and good beer too. ⓐ Michalská 10
☎ 02 5443 4038 ⓦ www.kristian.sk 🕒 11.00–00.00

Phones

Local, national and international calls can be made from call boxes in the street, in post offices and in some underpasses using coins or phonecards. Some internet cafés also offer cheap international

TELEPHONING SLOVAKIA

Slovakia's country code is 421. Bratislava's provincial area code, 02, must be dialled before all phone numbers, even for local calls. Mobile phone numbers here are easily recognisable as they all begin with 09.

TELEPHONING ABROAD

To dial abroad from Slovakia, dial 00, followed by the country code and then the number. Country codes: UK 44; Republic of Ireland 353; USA and Canada 1; Australia 61; New Zealand 64; South Africa 27.

calls. Discount calling cards such as **Telecard** (www.telecard.sk) enable you to call with up to 70 per cent discount overseas from anywhere in the world. If you are in Bratislava for any length of time, pick up a local pre-paid SIM card for your mobile. Local networks: **Orange** (W www.orange.sk), **T-Mobile** (W www.t-mobile.sk) and **Telefónica O$_2$ Slovakia** (www.o2.com).
International information 12 149
National information 1181
Yellow Pages W www.yellowpages.sk

Post
The **main post office** is at Nám SNP 35 (W www.slposta.sk
07.00–20.00 Mon–Fri, 07.00–18.00 Sat, 09.00–14.00 Sun).
Postboxes are orange.

ELECTRICITY
Slovakia's electricity supply is 220 volts. Plugs have two round pins, so UK electrical devices will need an adaptor. Visitors from the USA will also need a transformer.

TRAVELLERS WITH DISABILITIES
Bratislava was not designed to be and has not yet been updated to be accessible to those with disabilities. Some public transport needs to be stepped up into, and almost every major attraction and sight has innumerable steps. Presumably, as with other countries new to the EU, this will slowly change. Hotels usually do have rooms suitable for those with special needs. Ironically, persons with disabilities can enter most museums free of charge, but sadly many locations involve climbing up steep stairs.

TOURIST INFORMATION

If you're in search of tours, printed matter or just some general advice on making the most of your stay, visit one of Bratislava's helpful tourist information offices:

Main tourist information office ⓐ Klobúčnicka 2 ⓣ 02 5443 3715 ⓦ www.bkis.sk ⓛ 08.30–18.00 Mon–Fri, 09.00–16.00 Sat, 10.00–15.00 Sun, Oct–May; 08.30–19.00 Mon–Fri, 09.00–17.00 Sat, 10.00–17.00 Sun, June–Sept

NEWS & LISTINGS

Press International newsagents sell all the major international daily, weekly and monthly titles. Various venues stock magazines such as *City Guide Bratislava*, *Favourite Places* and *Enjoy Bratislava*. There's also an English monthly guide, *What's On Bratislava and Slovakia* (costing €1.50) and Slovak-language listings (easy to read nonetheless) *Club agenda* and *Kam do mesta*. The *Slovak Spectator* (ⓣ 02 5923 3300 ⓦ www.spectator.sk) is the country's only English language newspaper and is printed each Monday.

For maps and guides, visit the **Kníhkupectvo Academia bookstore** (ⓐ Štúrova 9 ⓣ 0905 479 818 ⓛ 08.00–18.30 Mon–Fri, 09.00–12.30 Sat ⓝ Tram: 1, 11, 12, 14).

Twin City Journal (ⓦ www.twincityjournal.eu) is an excellent monthly magazine in German, English and Slovakian listing what's on in Bratislava and Vienna. It is available in Bratislava from the tourist information offices.

Airport ☎ 02 4363 0306 ⏰ 09.00–18.00 Mon–Sat,
12.00–18.00 Sun

Passenger port @ Fajnorovo nábr 2 ☎ 02 5273 1602 ⏰ 09.00–15.00
Mon–Fri, 10.00–15.00 Sat & Sun, May–Oct

Railway station ☎ 02 5249 5906 ⏰ 08.00–19.00 Mon–Fri,
09.00–17.00 Sat & Sun, June–Sept; 09.00–17.00 Mon–Fri,
09.00–14.00 Sat & Sun, Oct–May

BACKGROUND READING

It's not just historically that the Slovak Republic has played
second fiddle to ruling nations and neighbouring Czechs.
In literature, too, Czech authors remain dominant – but
that's not to say the Slovaks have no voice.

For an insight into the Slovak oral storytelling tradition,
look no further than *Slovak Tales for Young and Old*, a true sum
of its parts. Tales were collected and edited by Pavol Dobšinský,
modernised by Peter Strelinger, translated by Lucy Bednar and
illustrated by Martin Benka, one of Slovakia's most famous artists.

The works of Janko Kráľ, Ján Kalinčiak and Jozef Cíger-Hronský
are also worth reading.

Emergencies

EMERGENCY NUMBERS

There are separate numbers for the police, fire and ambulance services, but the international emergency number ☎ 112 will get you through to an operator who will then direct your call to the service you require.

Ambulance ☎ 155   **Fire and rescue service** ☎ 150
City police ☎ 159   **State police** ☎ 158   **Traffic police** ☎ 154

MEDICAL SERVICES

Pharmacists are well known for being able to treat common ailments, but the real trick is conveying your problem if it isn't something that can safely be pointed at. *Lekáreň* (pharmacies) have the green cross sign.

Emergency medical treatment is available free of charge to British citizens to a certain extent. For repatriation or an air ambulance, for example, you will need to pay or have insurance.

The following are the most central hospitals in the area:
Nemocnica Staré Mesto ⓐ Mickiewiczova 13 ☎ 02 5729 0111
Nemocnica s poliklinikou ⓐ Ružinovská 6 ☎ 02 4823 4114
Nemocnica s poliklinikou ⓐ Limbová 5 ☎ 02 5954 1111

POLICE

If you are robbed or lose some property, you should report it to the police. State policemen wear green uniforms, and drive green and white cars. City policemen are in blue uniforms, drive white cars and have limited powers. The **two central police stations** are

EMERGENCY PHRASES

Help!	**Fire!**	**Stop!**
Pomoc!	Požiar!	Stop!
Pomots!	*Po-jar!*	*Stop!*

Call an ambulance/a doctor/the police/the fire service!
Volaj pohotovosť/lekára/políciu/požiarnikov!
Vo-lay po-ho-to-vos-t/le-kaa-ra/po-lee-tsy-u/po-zhiar-nee-kov!

at Špitálska 14 (☎ 09610 11111) and Obchodná 42 (☎ 02 5273 3817), where you may or may not find someone speaking English.

EMBASSIES & CONSULATES
Australian and New Zealand visitors are looked after by the British Embassy (see UK, below).
Canada @ Carlton Courtyard and Savoy Buildings, Mostová 2 ☎ 02 5920 4031 🕒 08.30–12.00, 13.30–16.30
Republic of Ireland @ Carlton Courtyard and Savoy Buildings, Mostová 2 ☎ 02 5930 9611 🌐 www.embassyofireland.sk
South African Honorary Consulate @ Révova 27 ☎ 02 5441 7841
UK @ Panská 14–16 ☎ 02 5998 2000 🌐 www.britishembassy.sk 🕒 08.30–17.00 Mon–Thur, 08.30–16.00 Fri (08.30–14.00 Fri, June–Aug)
USA @ Hviezdoslavovo nám ☎ 02 5443 3338. Emergency only: 0903 703 666 🌐 www.slovakia.usembassy.gov 🕒 08.00–16.30 Mon–Fri